Religion That Works

SERMONS OF PRACTICAL CHRISTIAN LIFE

By
S. M. SHOEMAKER, Jr.

*Rector of Calvary Church in
New York*

With an Introduction by
ALBERT PARKER FITCH, D.D.
*Minister, Park Avenue Presbyterian
Church, New York City*

NEW YORK   CHICAGO
Fleming H. Revell Company
LONDON AND EDINBURGH

BOOKS
BY S. M. SHOEMAKER, JR.

CHILDREN OF THE SECOND
BIRTH

RELIGION THAT WORKS

A YOUNG MAN'S VIEW OF
THE MINISTRY

REALIZING RELIGION

New York: 158 Fifth Avenue
Chicago: 851 Cass Street
London: 21 Paternoster Square
Edinburgh: 99 George Street

To
A. S. R.

INTRODUCTION

I AM not fond of reading sermons. Most of those which live in speech die in print; many more have never lived at all. But all the addresses, contained in this volume, I have read with profit and two of them, at least, I shall always remember.

For here are genuine convictions set forth with clarity and vigor. Here are the words of one who has found, for himself and others, the dynamic of a personal religion. On the basis of that experience he speaks to the world of here and now as we find it in our own American life in a great city. He puts down what one man thinks we ought to know about God and Man and Sin and the Gospel of Jesus Christ.

There is life in these pages. May they bring life to those who read them.

ALBERT PARKER FITCH.

Park Avenue Presbyterian Church Manse,
New York City.

CONTENTS

I

WHAT IF I HAD BUT ONE SERMON TO PREACH?

"This is life eternal, that they should know thee the only true God, and him whom thou didst send, even Jesus Christ."—John 17:3.

IT is a moving and sobering experience to try to make ready a sermon in which one attempts to say out the core of what one has found really important, really vital, in what one has learned about life, and the place of Christianity in it—to cut down the trivial and incidental, and to say the things one feels sure about, and believes everlastingly to matter to human beings.

If I had but one sermon to preach, I should first want to take a fresh look into the revealed heart of God. I believe the greatest window ever opened on the Eternal is the seventeenth chapter of St. John. There you will find set out before you the things Jesus thought about in the hour of His crisis: His faith and His fears, His values and His aims. He sees life in terms of a network of relationships between His Father, Himself, and those who have been given Him out of the world. That chapter is filled with personal pronouns. And in one great sentence He seems to give to us the sum and heart of the whole matter: " This is life eternal, that they

should know thee the only true God, and him whom
thou didst send, even Jesus Christ."

Now I should want to speak first about the
homesickness of the human soul for God. Life
does not furnish its own interpretation, the world
does not provide its own meaning. The world of
sense is well enough until our spirit is awake: but
the moment we awake, we feel a lonely sense of
uneasiness. The wider awake we become, the
sharper is the sense of incompleteness. Within
myself, within all men who have revealed to me
their own real interior life, I find a spiritual instinct, buried as deep within our natures as any
physical instinct can ever possibly be. The life
of sense cannot satisfy it, the glare of education
cannot reason it out for us. My work has carried
me behind the scenes in a good many lives, back
into the recesses where men really live: and I never
come back from that kind of an excursion without
a profounder conviction that I do not need to create
spiritual interest and craving—that has been cared
for long before.

There is a great phrase for this, early in the
fourth Gospel, where it is written, " That was the
true light that lighteth every man." That light
may shine in conscience, intuition, imagination,
beauty, the sense of the " numinous " or divine in
the world. This interpretation means that there is
a connection between the historic Christ and a
man's interior longing and aspiration: a practical
working identity between Him and our enlightened
consciences. If we were what that interior incompleteness craves for, we should be like Christ. And

the nearer we become like Him, and through Him
reach the Father, the more fully is that intense and
invisible longing satisfied and completed, so that
whatever happens to the outward life, the inward
life is rich and vivid and believing.   St. Augustine's
great saying for this is familiar to you all: " Thou
hast made us for Thyself, and our hearts are restless till they find rest in Thee."   The admission of
that fact is the first step, I think, to a genuine solution of the problem of life.   We are homesick as
we stand.

If I had but one sermon to preach, I should
want to say also that all of us at one time or other
thwart and disobey that spiritual nature within us.
We sin.   We live in a generation that loves to feed
itself on cheerful evasions of so sharp and con-
demning a word as sin—which calls our mis-
doings by nicer, softer words, explaining them by
psychological processes and names which take all
the responsibility out of our actions.   To call those
acts, and the condition of mind out of which they
spring, by the name of sin is to say that we are free
and independent moral beings, that we did not have
to act thus and could have done otherwise.   I want
an explanation of why it is that after I have dis-
obeyed the call of God within me, there comes an
immediate self-judgment and self-reproach which
is not scared off because somebody tells me I
have merely inherited a moral taboo: and why it
is that when I have sinned, prayer and peace are
both impossible.

Now, there has got to be some provision for that
fact in us, and some solution of the problem raised

by it. I don't only want a way of life: there have
been a thousand sages to say things that corre-
spond with my inner ethical sense. If Jesus could
provide only a way of life, He would stand on a
level with Confucius and Moses and Socrates. I
need redemption, not maxims. There is a rift
through my soul because of sin—a split, a division
in my nature. He who denies that for me is like a
doctor who denies mortal sickness when it is there.
It wants a tremendous cure. The more one thinks
about sin, the more absurdly inadequate appear the
current philosophies with their foolish faith in our
power to pull ourselves up by our own boot-straps.
I need help from without. I need salvation. I
need the Cross. And "the Cross is the medicine
of the world."

Now, there is another fact as inescapable as the
fact of sin, though our generation needs to learn it
over again, and that is the fact of conversion. It is
possible for a human soul to be lifted into a region
hitherto undiscovered, where the rift is healed,
where the disunity is harmonized, where peace
takes the place of pain, and strength of weakness,
and where one begins to live Life with a capital L.
The kind of thing that happened to St. Paul is happening still. Divided and unhappy people are con-
stantly being unified by what we call conversion.
The blessed news of the Christian Gospel is that
nobody needs to rest content with being what he is.
Utterly without regard for anybody's gifts or limitations, Jesus held out to us a Gospel that begins,
"Whosoever . . ."

Now, you know as well as I do, that we have left

conversion, on the whole, to the rescue missions and
the Salvation Army.   God be praised for all they
are doing.   But it is one of the deepest convictions
of my life that conversion needs to be put within
reach of privileged and educated people, that Park
Avenue needs it as badly as the Bowery, and that
thousands upon thousands of ordinary church-
people have been kept outside the real joy and
power of the Christian religion because the Christian Church has been too ready to accept them as
they are, and has hardly believed its own Invincible
Christ is strong enough to convert the complacent
and the prosperous and the intelligent.   I am
through catering to the intellectual vanity of this
generation, and I am through being satisfied with
lip-service in well-to-do church members.

Last night I was called to a hotel in this city,
where a young man who had made wreck of his life
had been drinking steadily for a week.   In despair
about himself, he asked for help.   And from ten-
thirty to one we talked.   I told him of the Christ
who could save men like himself: and hungrily and
eagerly he listened.   But years back a clergyman
had failed him in the hour of his need: he had made
a serious mistake in school, and the clergyman shut
his door on him as a protest.   And he carried in his
heart a raging hatred for church-hypocrisy, which
had kept him from Holy Communion and any
church service since he was a boy.   He was persuaded to come to Holy Communion this morning
at the early service, and it was the first time in
fifteen years.   And as his soul wrestled in a life and
death struggle, some woman kneeling piously be-

hind him was talking to her neighbour about
whether she had gone to such and such a show last
night! I don't know who that woman is, and I
don't want to know. But it is a sad pass when a
human soul coming to Christ for rescue from sin
and self, must be interrupted by that kind of a
Christian.

The world does not need an awakening any more
than the Church does. It was to an educated religious gentleman that Jesus said, " Ye must be
born again." That imperative is a judgment
against those who withstand conversion. But it is
a hope held out to those fearful and self-depreci-
ating people who do not think themselves capable
of conversion. The new life begins by utter self-
dedication to the will of God. All of us can do
that, and must.

If I had but one sermon to preach, I should want
to say to you all that I believe enormously in the
possibility of a guided life, influenced and led at
every step by the Holy Spirit. Conversion is the
beginning, not the ending, of an experience of God.
That experience continues when we use all the
means Jesus put at our disposal for continuation—
prayer, the Scriptures, the Church and the Sacraments, Christian fellowship and worship. There is
a kind of Christianity which sticks faithfully by
the precepts, a kind of new legalism, and good so
far as it goes. But I believe God meant each one
of us to experience a fresh and personal relationship to Him which becomes creative and original.
Many situations in my life are not covered by the
Sermon on the Mount. I need special guidance and

illumination. The prophets of Israel had it. The apostles had it. Where is it gone to in this age? We believe in the Holy Spirit as we believe in some dead human character: he was once, but he is gone. The deepest need of our age, the cure for most of our back-door attempts to establish communication with the other world, is a rediscovery of the Holy Spirit.

What infinite possibilities of learning the will of God, through communion with Him, may lie ahead of us, who can dare to imagine? Here, surely, is the realm in which unbelievable development is still possible. Science, with a long face, says, " Man is done evolving physically and intellectually: we have not gone beyond the Greeks in body or brain." And religion, scanning a far horizon with hope in her eyes, says, " Man has scarcely begun to evolve spiritually: he is to-day spiritually where he was physically when his eyes were light-spots and his spine a piece of gristle. And beyond him stretch unseen and unimagined capacities for traffic with the other world." It is not the scientists who deny, but the spiritual experimenters who believe in first-hand touch with God, who are the real progressives in our world. The most advanced type of human being I know is represented by this sentence from a friend, just put into my hands: " I feel the beginning of the experience of a day when prayer runs under and through everything."

If this were the last sermon I were going to preach, I should lay upon you all your duty to cry out to men in darkness that this is The Way. Because it has been done badly, because some have been offended by it, we have tended to forget and omit evangelism altogether. In the days of religion's youth and vigour and health, when it is potent enough to form men's minds and transform their lives, you will find it carrying them far out beyond self-conscious concern about what others will say or think of them: they have found the Messiah, and it is heavy upon their hearts that they must call out to the world, " Come and see! " that they may find Him also. It would not be an intrusion to call to a caravan in the desert that you know where water is: and we are here as in a desert, where the souls of men shrivel and go to dust for lack of the Water of Life. Let it be done with wisdom and tact, with sympathy and good humour and seasoned with salt—but let it be done!

I suspect that if you and I knew that our end were near, we should regret nothing so much as to look back upon the lost opportunities of hungry human souls to whom we might have spoken of the all-satisfyingness of the Christ, but to whom we did not speak because we were afraid. Touching lives one by one is fascinating business, and involves some of the most rewarding and beautiful human relationships that can possibly arise. But its motive does not lie in its interest or its reward, but in its urgent need. We may think we are emancipated in this generation; but for all our freedom, we are making a worse fist of life than men made when they believed in God. And we need a host of men and women who believe that, to go forth and say it in the highways and byways of the earth.

If you have found The Way, tell men so—otherwise they will probably never find it.

And I should want to say a particular word about the amazing adequacy of Christ. He is alive, and He is a Person, and He is within reach of you and me. Of the best life that has been lived for twenty centuries, He is the author. The best men and women I know owe everything to Him. He does not save them from the hard knocks that life brings to us all, surely by some design: but He saves them from bitterness, from rebelliousness, from the feeling of destitution and futility. When trouble comes, they do not worry, but rather wait for His full purpose to emerge through the trial. That much I see in others. And what I see for them, that I have experienced for myself. I am not old, and outwardly life has slipped along smoothly and happily for me: but you know that no man can live at all, in his own or others' experience, without inward struggle, battle, temptation, suffering. I can say to you without reserve or quibbling, that Jesus Christ satisfies. He puts a purpose into life it never had before. He shares all its loads and its perplexities. He literally and actually stoops into my life to give me help in the hour of temptation, as often as I let Him come. He makes people happy, not with the hard indifference to trouble of the Stoic, not with the soft indifference of the professional optimist, but with that joy of His own which caused Him to cry out, " Be of good cheer—I have overcome the world."

And because of His adequacy here, I trust Him in what He says of all that lies before. I find Him mistaken in nothing He said about this life: I trust Him about the next. I believe that one day I shall face Him, and give account to Him of the deeds done in the body. And if that be so, it is going to alter all my way of travelling through this world. If I had but this one sermon to preach, I think I should surely want to warn against the prevalent view of life which makes this world the centre. Life is short, and quantitatively unimportant. But life is decisive, and qualitatively immensely impor-portant. For there takes place in this life a set of character, a drift of spirit, which there is no good ground for believing will cease to obtain when the last river is crossed. We shall be when we land yonder what we were when we left this shore. Through unending ages, I believe, the love of God will pursue a soul to the utmost confines of this universe to fetch it back to Him: but souls are free to choose, and free to refuse. They miss God here, and they may reject Him forever. The soul that permanently refuses God chooses hell instead.

I believe that hell is the lasting absence of God—that is what I understand by it, and I see no Christian warrant for a sentimental evasion of believing in it. It is the natural evolution of a rebellious soul. We want everything else to go according to strict law, but we want God to intervene suddenly when we see where the path we have been treading leads us, and to save everybody regardless. We are tampering with spiritual laws in our easy modern forgetfulness of the wages of sin. God is not pitchforking souls into hell—they are pitchforking themselves when they refuse His salvation from

themselves and their sin. You don't grow hya-
cinths out of onions: and souls are not born into
the presence of God in heaven who have all their
lives fled His presence on earth. I am not com-
mending a religion of fear, but simply a religion of
fact, and not of fancy, as too many choose for
themselves to-day. This world is the brief school-
time of an everlasting spirit: and we need to take
it seriously for the training, but not as if it were
the world which matters most.

But that " eternal life " which goes on in the infinite ages of God does not begin with death, it
begins with the acceptance of God in Jesus Christ.
" This is life eternal, that they should know thee,
the only true God, and him whom thou didst send,
even Jesus Christ." God is knowable in Christ:
and what that acquaintance brings to us is a present sense of our immortality, in a life which is so
good that we feel within us it is indestructible.

There is but one final thing I would want to say.
To some of us that relationship is an aspiration
unrealized. We do not know Him, nor have we
really found Him. And I believe the trouble lies
here: we have not surrendered ourselves to Him.
There is something within us He hates, and we will
not let it go. There is a plan He has for us bigger
than our own plan, and we are afraid of it. Somewhere we hold back. Somewhere we keep control
of our own destiny. Let go! Abandon yourself to
Him. Say to Him, " Not my will but Thine be
done." Live it. Pray for it. Put yourself at His
disposal for time and for eternity. And if your
experience is anything like mine has been, you will

find that Jesus gives to life a zest and a glory, a peace and a purpose, which He only can give. If these glimpses of eternal life which come to us through Him are pledges of what we may know perpetually when the shadows flee away, I want to live forever. And by the mercy of God in Christ by His gift of eternal life, by the atoning sacrifice of His Cross, I believe I shall.

Let us pray:

O God, who didst send Thy Son into the world to make Thyself known to us in ways we could understand: Lay upon us a sense of urgency about our religion, lest in apathy and dull acceptance we miss the best Thou hast for us. Waken all the spiritual possibilities within us. Help us to give all we have to Thee, and to help Thee build the Kingdom. And in Thy mercy bring us at the last into Thy presence, to worship and enjoy Thee forever. Through the merits of Thy Son, Jesus Christ our Saviour. Amen.

II

THE NECESSITY OF CHRIST

"No man hath seen God at any time; the only begotten Son, who is in the bosom of the Father, he hath declared him."—John 1:18.

I SPEAK to you to-day upon the Necessity of Christ.

One may believe that the reason why Christ came was the sin of man. God had tried all through the long path of human history to make Himself known. Through dim heathen ceremonies, through the haunting fears of animism, through pagan mythology; and then through the law and the prophets of the Hebrews, through Abraham and Moses, through Isaiah and Hosea, God had been sending out reminders to the human race. But all failed because of the stubbornness of man, his wilfulness and his independence. And " Christ Jesus came into the world to save sinners "—there is scriptural authority for this view, and it commends itself to every man's common sense.

But I do not believe that is the *only* reason for the coming of Christ. It is quite possible that, even if we had done what we should and been what we ought, Christ would nevertheless have come. For all we know, it may have been part of the eternal purpose of God that, " in the fullness of time," He should send forth His Son into the world. I believe that there are things which God wanted to say to us human beings which could not be said save through such an one as Christ, and that He was necessary in God's whole scheme, and not merely a remedy for the apparent failure of God to make men remember Him.

I want to take up with you certain points which seem to me to necessitate a human revelation of God, a historic expression of God in terms of human life. There are facts in our experience which, without Christ, seem to me to remain unsolved and insoluble problems.

In the first place, God is hard to know. There is a widely-known preacher of very liberal thinking who has said recently that it is presumptuous of Christians to think that they can know God. This gentleman has turned agnostic, and feels that we cannot know. But I would like to remind him that Christianity itself is agnostic about God, apart from the revelation of Christ. " No man hath seen God at any time," says St. John—and I take it that he means something more than physical sight which could have no application here: he means, I believe, that in His final nature, apart from authentic revelation of Himself, God is obscure and unknowable. The mystery of life lies too heavy upon us all not to know how desolate a mood that sentence may express: " No man hath seen God at any time." There is ruthlessness in natural creation which is hard to reconcile with a good God. There is impersonality in the laws of the natural world to which we are all made subject. The mechanism of the modern is only the fatalism of the ancient in a different dress, the Anangke of the Greek, the Kismet of the Mohammedan. There are times when we seem to be caught as a wild thing in a trap. Little children suffer for others' sins, and men hate and fight, and there is the ever-lasting problem of the dreadfully poor. What kind of a God is God? That is the ever-present problem of life.

And even if you say that the force of the universe is personal, in the sense that there is intelligence and will in that Force, how much does He care for us, whether we rise or sink? What communication is possible between us? Are there secrets in His keeping which I may learn if I listen? Is He force, or is He Father? Those questions, without Christ, are left permanently unanswered. But if Christ is the revelation of God, if God feels towards us as Christ does; if He represents the perfect character of God completely expressed in human and understandable terms, then, for all that our liberal friend may say, we do know God. Him whom we have been ignorantly worshipping, Him Christ declares unto us. The perfection of Christ's own life and character is the best seal that He is the revelation of God. What can you think of God as being, which Christ is not? What further perfection does your imagination glimpse which is not in Christ? And can you not say, with St. John, that " the only begotten Son, who is in the bosom of the Father, he hath declared Him "?

Not only is God hard to know, but life is hard to meet successfully. People are always at sea about what they shall love most: and from that comes the perplexity of mind which does not know how to act. We have no basic values, therefore we have no standards, therefore we have no principle of living and acting. How many people have you known who, with a gesture of new-won freedom, have flung religion to the winds, and for a few months or years gone along without it? And then comes wonder. What *is* right? What *is* worth working for? What meaning *has* life, after all?

I talked but this week with a man who was long ago a member of this church, and now feels no need to go anywhere. Yet he spends much time away from his wife and children because of small irritation. And he talked to me shyly about his own "confusion of mind." Life *is* confusing without Christ: for we know neither what to believe in nor what principle to act upon. There are mysterious and seemingly contradictory experiences which come to all of us: and we do not know our way through them. And I suppose that what we do at a time like that is to look about to those who seem to be meeting life more successfully than we are. We see through the failures of nine-tenths of what people call life: and in the other tenth we see a glimmer of meaning. From them we seek sympathy, or advice, or just strength to lean on. But there is no permanent cure here. For we shall be again in trouble. Must we be everlastingly restless, always turning to someone else for a second-hand solution? What makes us turn to those other people? It is generally that, as we say, they have " got something." That is an evasive phrase for saying they believe in and trust God. They generally trust God as they have come to know Him in Christ. Why not go direct to the Source? Why not say that Christ offers the only ideal for man that fits in this world and covers all the cases that can arise?

And it is not enough merely to *tell* about an ideal. The world's sages from the beginning have done that. But Christ also embodies that ideal perfectly in Himself. He is not pointing to a distant height while He stands Himself just where we stand. He began just where we are and made the climb: but He stands upon that height and calls down to us to come up, for He knows the ascent is possible, because He has made it. That is the only kind of an ideal that is worth much to us—not only a realizeable ideal, but a realized ideal, embodied in a perfect life. I say that Christ is utterly necessary to give mankind light on his path.

Third, sin is hard to overcome. For there are times when I see light on my path, and know just where I ought to go: but I do not go. I wilfully go in another direction. And when I know the will of God and choose my own instead, that is sin.

The world has its cheap solutions. One of them is that everybody else sins, too. And that is a lying solution, for some have found the path: and even if the majority have not, there is no more peace in herd-sin than in individual sin.

Another solution is that we do enough good to make up for it in the long run: John may get drunk, but John is good-hearted, and God will forget the getting drunk. It is the solution of a morally foggy mind. It is ethically no solution at all. For when we sit down alone and face ourselves as we really are, we know that sin is a barrier between us and our own best, and between us and God. It is a definite problem which we consider as a problem except when we are trying to evade it for self-justification. And we need a solution for it.

TRANSITION

Christ offers us three things. The first is *forgiveness* for the past. He holds out the heart of God as willing to forgive anyone who comes in honest penitence and says he is sorry and means to stop. He makes matters right between us and Him. As a friend said to me this week, " The past is *gone*."

The second is power to stop sinning. None of us does very well at overcoming sin, but when we do, we know that it has not been all our own doing. Co-operation, yes, but not our own sole effort. For " every virtue we possess, and every victory won, and every thought of holiness, are His alone."

And the third is, the *Cross* to make up for the mass of unatoned, unforgiven, unwashed sin. There is a heap of it. Some I have not recognized. Some I have not had heart to confront and deal with. Some I committed with Christ almost standing by. I can do nothing about it. There is absolutely no excuse for it. I cannot honestly say I tried not to do it. Nothing in me can handle that sin. Only the stooping and infinite mercy of God, taking my sin upon Him, can deal with it, shrive it, obliterate it. (The Cross is the only solution. And without it the revelation of God in Christ and the Ideal of man in Christ would leave a terrible incompleteness. Christ alone holds in His hand the key and the cure for sin.) Plenty of sages, with ideals to offer. Plenty of good people, with advice. (But only one Saviour, to offer a solution for human sin.)

3. And finally, death looks like the end. It is all very well for people to talk about caterpillars turning into butterflies: and the return of the springtime, with the sprouting leaves upon the trees. But butterflies die, and trees die: and while the energy may go off into some other sphere, according to some law of the conservation of energy, that is not much comfort. People may talk about living on in posterity, or the fame of a good name: but that is a pale immortality, a substitute and cheat for eternal life. We belong to the animal kingdom: and it looks as though dead things stay dead. We shall never know again, I suppose, the withering devastation of death in the ancient pagan world. I have seen some of it remaining in China and India. Whatever survival was believed in in the pagan world was shadowy and filmy existence, the spawn of a hopeless hope. There was nothing whatever to authenticate it but the wish of men. (And for most of us, it is not a cheerful prospect that death is the end of all things. A few people with more bravado than brains talk about meeting it philosophically and the rest, but normal human beings wish for immortality, and crave it as deeply as they crave anything in life.)

Now, Christ brings a solution here. He sets going in men's lives here a quality which He called " eternal life," which was the product of a relationship between us and His Father through Him. He believed that that life went on in the infinite ages of

Resurrection is the solution ✝

God unbroken and ever unfolding in new riches. This might be merely a hope also, except for one fact: and that fact is His own death and resurrection. Lord Acton, the British historian, said that the resurrection of Christ was one of the best-authenticated facts in history. Never mind now whether body rose with spirit: the indubitable fact is that the apostles were in touch afresh with the Personality which had left them, to all physical appearance, on the Cross. They gathered together again, picked up the bits of a movement shattered by His two days in the grave, and set out to conquer the world with the faith in life after death. And that was the sure part of their creed which utterly swept the pagan world, long dark with despair about the future. (I do not want a hope, I want a well-authenticated assurance of life to come. Anybody can wish: but I want evidence. And Christ brought that evidence and laid it before me, woven into the very vitals of the early Church, by His own presence and risen power in their midst. Death is not the end, but the beginning. Christ alone is our final witness.)

(I hope that what I have said may help to convince you of the central necessity of Christ in faith.) There are those who say that Christ did not think of Himself except as a way to God, and that He put God in the first place. So, I think, He did; but He also said that He was one with His Father, and that He was Way and Truth and Life, and Bread of Life, and Door, and Good Shepherd, and Resurrection and Life, and Son of God. " No man cometh unto the Father but by me " lays an emphasis upon

Christ as great as that upon God. If God cannot be fully known and approached apart from Christ, which I believe is not a dogma but an experience, then there is not much difference between Them. When learned modern theologians say they are baffled by the Nicene Creed with its outworn metaphysics, " begotten of the Father before all worlds, God of God, light of light, very God of very God, begotten not made, being of one substance with the Father by whom all things were made,"(I should like to presume to tell them that it means one very great big thing, and that is, that there is not much difference between God and Christ.) Now, if they do not believe that, let them come out and say so. But let them be honest, and stop talking about creedal obscurity, when the fog is in their own minds. (The kind of Christianity which has captured the world has not been a Christianity of ethics, or of faith in God, or of social righteousness alone—it has been a Christianity which emphasized Christ and exalted Him and prayed to Him and found Him a living Lord of present experience, and sought to have the kind of experiences reproduced in them which He had in His own life.)

And so I ask you to focus your minds, not so much upon His philosophy or His view of God, or even His teachings, but rather upon Christ Himself. We cannot be too much concerned with Him. The greatest servants the world has ever seen have been those whose minds revolve round Him with a kind of holy pre-occupation, who cannot let Him alone, whose gaze always comes to a full stop when their eyes meet Him. From that creative relationship arises more kindness, more ingenious human service, more moral power, more spiritual insight, and more sweetness of life, than from anywhere else in all the world.

It is not enough to know the centrality of Christ in Christian thinking; we must make Him central in our planning and our working and our spending. He is not necessary to the wide world unless He is necessary to us. It is a dangerous thing to put Him at the centre of history and not put Him also at the centre of our lives.

Let us to-day, in thankfulness for what He has done for us and for all men, enthrone Him again in the high place of our hearts.

III

WHAT IS UNBELIEF?

" And he marvelled because of their unbelief."—Mark 6:6.

PROBABLY no generation ever paid such high honour to unbelief as our own. There are a great many people to-day who almost automatically think better of the intellectual integrity of the man who disbelieves than of the man who believes. Since Tennyson said:

> *" There lives more faith in honest doubt,*
> *Believe me, than in half the creeds,"*

every little two-by-four sceptic has taken it to apply to himself, and set his faithlessness upon a higher pinnacle for admiration than the faith of Isaiah or of St. John the Divine. Unbelief is a very popular personage today, and I think we may do well to look a little into his ancestry and his character.

Go back in your imagination to a scene outside the village church in the city of Nazareth. A young Man of this town has just come back from a preaching and healing journey by the Lake of Galilee. Word has been brought back to the village of the extraordinary influence this Man has exerted, healing the sick, even raising the dead, calling men away from their livelihood to follow Him in His mission. These stories spread like

31

wildfire in an oriental village: and they are added to, and distorted and seen out of focus. A little family, without too much imagination, is a bit embarrassed at the fame of this Eldest Son; and they wish He would come home and let His mission alone—there is plenty of hard work to be done in Nazareth.

And on this Saturday morning a crowd of chatterers gather just after church, the village gossips, the half-sentimental, half-cruel group that makes up a popular crowd. The young Man has come home and preached in the village church. And because He was wise without being learned, and because He was spiritually powerful without being recognized before He left the village, and because He was nobody but one of themselves, " the carpenter, the Son of Mary," they were scandalized about Him. And there emanated from that crowd a cloud, a mist of unbelief as palpable as poison gas, an atmosphere of scepticism and devastating misgiving, so that all He would do was to heal a few sick folk—presumably in some quarter of the town where the air was clear, where those fumes of withering rejection had not been able to come.

But for those few unspoiled spots, where a green blade of unwithered faith stood upright, all Nazareth lay under a miasma of unbelief in the only Person that keeps Nazareth from oblivion. The words, the gestures, the silences of the muttering little crowd of gossipers spread like an unholy gas, from the very door of the village church.

" And he marvelled because of their unbelief."

What is unbelief? We think to-day that it means

intellectual unwillingness to swallow ancient doc-
trines. But there was no doctrine here. We think
that it means the dark conclusion of men who have
looked life square in the face and say that it is in-
sensate and meaningless. But here was no hard
philosophical reasoning. We think that unbelief is
the attitude of a proud Hindu or Confucianist towards Christianity, for which, with perverted toler-
ance, we admire him and in which we encourage
him. But here was no comparison, and no judgment laid against far-distant men. We like to keep
unbelief in the upper story of our natures, and to
think that it is the product of reason alone: because
that feeds our pride just where this generation most
wants it to be fed. But this unbelief had other
factors in it than sound reasoning.

Now, I want to stop long enough to pay my re-
spects to all those who have genuine intellectual
difficulty with Christianity. The new world has
created new problems. We cannot, if we would,
look out on life with the outlook which men had
half a century ago. Let me say that I have no fear
for Christianity if you will make a complete intellectual investigation of it, historically, philosophically, psychologically and, above all, practically.
But I have a great many fears that you will be
deceived about your own intellectuality, as thousands are to-day deceived about theirs. There is
more in the make-up of common human unbelief
than pure and honest reasoning.

What was the unbelief of that crowd in Nazareth? *Unbelief was the rejection of spiritual power
in the plain face of that power*. It didn't come out

of their heads, but out of their hearts and their attitudes and their customs and their purses, and
right up out of the inward vitals of them. There
was mighty little that was intellectual in it: but all
the rest of a wrongly-based nature rose up to stand
against this Man. Unbelief was the refusal to
recognize and to accept a spiritual power whose
force was manifested to them where they could all
see it. This was not something which their minds
forced them to reject: it was something their consciences forced them to receive, but they would not.
Faith would not have meant believing in something
they could not see, but accepting something they
could see.

The primary factor in their unbelief was moral.
Be sure of this: that what Jesus " marvelled at "
you may put down for an unnecessary and an un-
natural thing. Do you remember when Jesus appeared to the eleven, after His resurrection, and
" upbraided them with their unbelief and hardness
of heart "? You may be sure that Jesus would not
rebuke an honest intellectual dissent. He must
have felt in them some quality for which they were
responsible, some moral obtuseness which kept
them from recognizing Him in the plain manifestation of His resurrection-power. It was no paltry
intellectual questioning which He felt, either after
the resurrection, or way back there in Nazareth:
He felt that the moral stubbornness and unrecep-
tiveness of these men was the predominant quality
of their unbelief. I shall never forget studying the
eighth chapter of St. John with a man whom I believe to be the most gifted preacher of this gener-

ation: and he called that chapter " a supernaturally acute analysis of the ultimate moral origin of unbelief." It is a striking and terrible phrase—" the ultimate moral origin of unbelief."

But the more I come into touch with unbelief, and see round it, and see behind it, the more do I believe in the judgment which lies wrapped in that phrase. I believe that all intellectual doubt is alloyed with moral factors. We do not come to any conclusions merely with our minds. The rest of our nature casts its vote in every decision. Sin is always calling to doubt, " Come over and help us." These two together will rob a man of all the spiritual conviction he has, if they can bind him between them. I have never met a perfect man, nor a man without some kind of moral twist in him. I believe that when a man's mind comes to deal with religion, it cannot suddenly slough off all the rest of him and become naked and honest mentality all at once. No—the rest of his nature will have its vote. And by as much as I have never found a *man* whose *life* was not alloyed with sin, by so much have I never found a man whose *mind* was not alloyed with sin in making its decisions. The profoundest scientist has prejudices, loves, temperament, dispositional tendencies, which affect all his work; and enter especially into all large judgments which he makes of life as a whole. All men sin.

Therefore, into the doubt of every man comes the weight of sin, pulling the scales towards unbelief. For unbelief and sin are sworn and congenital allies. If sin can make a man lose faith in God, it can have its own way with him. If doubt can make sin its ally, together they can rob him of God and wreck his life. There is a subtle and inevitable co-operation between these two. Unbelief may be honest, intellectually considered: but search your unbelief with honest scrutiny, and see what else you find tied to it, beside scrupulous intellectual fidelity to the facts!

Similarly, the way out of unbelief is moral as well as intellectual. Jesus said, "If any man willeth to do his will, he shall know." That is to say, " If any man will begin by living up to as much as he understands of the moral requisites of God, he will later, in the light of his experience, come to see straight intellectually." That is an experimental challenge, and it has been the experience of thousands upon thousands that it is an experiment which leads to truth for life. I may be quite unable to convince a man he is wrong in not believing in God or in the divinity of Christ: if I can get him to live according to the revealed will of the God in whom as yet he cannot believe, time will come when he will believe in that God and understand with his mind. A moral experiment is worth ten times an intellectual investigation in apprehending spiritual truth. Obedience is as much the organ of spiritual understanding as reason. Many people have come into a personal and living faith by trying the experiment which is implied in: " If any man willeth to do his will, he shall know."

Unbelief, therefore, is not naked intellectual doubt: it is compounded with moral refusal to proceed upon the evidence of the experience of others. It is as much a matter of temperament, oftentimes, as of reason. And it often has its seat more in the will than in the mind. Unbelief is the negative atmosphere, the unexpectant, unhopeful attitude. Christian Science is right so far: we do create an atmosphere conducive to creative progress, or hostile to it. The root of some unbelief is the spirit of " It can't be done."

It is unbelief to treat an old situation as though it could never be remedied. We are always thinking people cannot be changed—especially the people we know best, and whose qualities seem to be so rooted that they can never be altered. Frequently I come upon young men whose families have never given them any religion to speak of. They have gone off to school and heard about Christ as a new experience. Because it is new, it is sometimes more interesting to them than to those families who have been long exposed to it. Such a boy comes home, and wonders what would happen if his family should really understand about Christ. I talked with such a boy last week. And it was hard for him to realize that his father is plastic and changeable still. He is not the immovably set and unalterable human being he thinks of as his father —but is probably unsatisfied underneath a kind of success. But it is hard for that boy to think of his father in new ways. And it is hard to escape the binding and killing effect of that kind of unbelief. We all succumb to it whenever we regard anybody as hopeless and impossible to touch. God can touch anybody. Our own unfaith may make it impossible for God to do the work He wants to do through us.

It is unbelief when you are called upon to assume

a larger responsibility which is offered to you by others who know your capacity: and something within you quails and shivers and says: "No. I am not capable of it. I will fail." The very willingness to tackle it might have distended your own capacity. Many a man seems to undergo a fresh accession of ability when he begins a piece of work which is too large for him.

And it is unbelief when we are called to go through something, and we begin to waver and fear. We may know that we are going to lose someone who is very dear to us, or that we must face a long period of suffering, or separation. Something inside us crumples up and goes dead. We all know the sensation. And yet that very fear may paralyze the power which would have made it possible to go through with it. Unbelief isn't doubting some fact of long ago—unbelief is acting and feeling as though there were no God in the daily conduct of our lives. You can believe in miracles in the New Testament and the Old: but if you cannot believe in miracles in your own life, your faith is cold, intellectual assent; and not the warm and vibrant thing Christ meant faith to be.

It is unbelief when we are satisfied with second-best when we can aim at first. The kind of unbelief, which is my problem, is to think there are people who really cannot grasp or undergo the thing I mean by an experience of Christ. When I put anyone—old, conventional Christian, or weak, unconvinced unbeliever—outside the actual possibility of as deep an experience of Christ as I have known, that is unbelief.

When I am sometimes dreaming great things for this parish, and seeing in it potentially a great spiritual centre, where men and women may find held up the living Christ, and feel His Spirit amongst us, and find Him and be forever changed, and go forth bearing His message to the world, something whispers in my ear, " That's a day-dream. They will not really get what you mean. They will be just like every other crowd of church-people—no friendlier, no deeper, no realer than any others. Do not expect too much. Give them as much religion as will keep them coming to church and being decent citizens, but do not expect to make prophets out of them; for you cannot hope to do it." *That* is unbelief for me.

There *have* been congregations that have radiated the Spirit of Christ so that any chance comer felt it the moment he came in the door—congregations filled with real spiritual power. Against the evidence of facts rises up this mood, this misgiving, this fear out of some dark place in my own heart. And that doubt for me is sin—sin against which I have to fight as against any other sin. It is not a reasonable conclusion: faith enough on my part and on yours might achieve the miracle of an entirely Christian local church. When I doubt it, the fear arises, not from outside myself where I cannot control it, but from inside myself where I can.

It is unbelief when we see the power of Christ come wonderfully down into the life of another, and they say, " But that never can come to me." How do you know? Do you not close the door in the face of Christ when you say a thing like that, and

lock it when you persist in saying that the other
person is better equipped by temperament than
you, or does not have the baffling questions arise
that come to you? How do you know? Most honest people have intellectual difficulties with religion.
You are not alone. They have fought through their
doubts—why shouldn't you fight through yours?

I say that Jesus would not marvel at unbelief
unless unbelief were something which could be
dealt with as a problem, and did not need to be
accepted as a fate. Unbelief may be a way-station,
but it is not meant for a destination. There are
other factors in most of it than pure reason. And
by its own unwillingness to die, like a dead leaf,
and let a live thing come and take its place—by its
persistent demand to monopolize life, doubt usurps
the direction of life which ought to belong, until
God is found, to the conscience; and after God is
found, to Him.

It is no good being general. Let us come to grips
with the unbelief in our own lives—not the questioning of this or that miracle or point of theology
—those may need to wait till larger matters are set-
tled. I mean unbelief about God and life and the
goodness of the universe and the worthwhileness of
life. If you question here, ask yourself very honestly how much sin enters into your doubt—sin of
intellectual pride, sin of self-pity which loves to
think itself injured in an unjust cosmos, sin of lazi-
ness which will not really investigate, sin of fear
which will not face God lest He ask of us that which
we are unwilling to grant. I do not say this to con-
demn you, but to reveal you to yourselves. Be

quite honest whether this seems to you a wholly reasonable way to look at religion—or whether you are more like the crowd at Nazareth, whose unbelief was born and spread in the very place where Christ's power could have been proved and demonstrated. They would not give Him the chance to prove Himself. Is that what you are doing? Have you sought out people He has helped, and found out how it came? Or have you gone off skulking and said religion was all humbug and emotion?

Are you afraid of the demands of Christ? " Cold feet " have kept more people away from Christ than cold logic. It was that moral, responsible element in unbelief which Christ detected and despised in the crowd at Nazareth, and despises still. He says to our age, as He said to His own, with terrible exposure of sin as the root of unbelief: " Why do ye not understand my speech? Even because ye cannot hear my word. Ye are of your father the devil, and the lusts of your father it is your will to do. He was a murderer from the beginning, and standeth not in the truth because there is no truth in him." " Because there is no truth in him "—there stands Christ's exposure of the root and cause for much in us which masquerades as intellectual integrity. Somebody needs to take down this generation in the pride of its intellect, and humble it before God. This world is the small end of life. Knowledge of God is worth more than all the wisdom of the world. This age needs to know how much of its unbelief is conceit at the bottom.

Let us, then, lift up our eyes to the Christ, and

lay hold of every meaning we can find in Him. In Him are gathered up all the values which our best selves understand. Let us put aside abstract intellectual difficulties, and seek first a personal relationship to Him, in the light of which truth may break. Let us bring to Him, not only ourselves but our problems, not only our faith but our unbelief as well, saying with the centurion of old: " Lord, I believe. Help thou "—for there is none other to help—" mine unbelief."

Let us pray:

O God, who in all ages hast imparted Thyself to man and set alight the fire of faith in his heart: Grant to us the faith which comes from search. Cleanse our lives from all that negates and crushes out faith: fill them with the purity and honesty which fosters it. Search us for the evil which makes unbelief its friend, and drive it far from us. So that being willing, in all things, to do Thy will, we may know the truth which shall set us free, by the light of the Holy Spirit. Through Jesus Christ our Lord. Amen.

IV

THE MEANING OF SELF-SURRENDER

"Who then offereth willingly to consecrate himself this day unto Jehovah?"—I Chronicles 29:5.

THE meaning of self-surrender to God is the deepest meaning in all the experience of religion. There is something deep-hidden within us which makes us feel that, whatever God is, He is more ideal than we are, and that we shall tend to find our life by yielding it, in as nearly an absolute sense as possible, to the Ideal Power which we call God. The very earliest stirrings of faith in God at all carry with them some natural response of this sort. It is hard for us to think of God without thinking also of our duty towards Him, and it is impossible to conceive that duty in any vitally personal sense without the consciousness that we cannot begin to do it until we have first offered the whole of ourselves to God. Like human love, religion is impossible without the maximum of self-giving.

I am perfectly sure that self-surrender is for most people an unrealized aspiration. They feel the edges of it in great moments of joy or of sadness. Music stirs it in them, if they be susceptible to music. Art may do it, or a sunset sky. A great spoken word, or the convincing life of a saint—

there are a thousand possible stimuli to the thought of self-surrender to the Power of the universe. But this generally goes off into diffuse ether. The thing is mostly emotion which does not harness itself to something that needs to be done. It is fitful and unsustained. It is a glimpse we get into reality, that does not last long enough to become an abiding possession, a permanent attitude of obedience and trust and loving co-operation.

If I can to-day, I want to draw this thing out of the vague region where for most of us it resides, only occasionally invading our minds, and put it where it may become actual for us all. May I say to you, frankly and personally, that I was a missionary on foreign soil, with a Christian home, confirmation, many student conferences, and a decision to enter the ministry, behind me, before I ever saw the luminous depths, the liberating power, of the experience of self-surrender? My brethren, these things ought not so to be; and it is one of the great resolves of my ministry that they shall not be where, by preaching and talking in season and out of season, upon the reality of this experience, I can prevent them from being. It is a lamentable thing that in our religious instruction, and our preaching, we can hit upon so many peripheral and secondary things, while Christian people go through their lives without knowing that this central experience is possible for them.

William James has told us that people belong to one of two types, the once-born, or the twice-born type. Emerson was a type of the first, a mind always at unity with itself, with little consciousness of duality or division, which holds communion with the Absolute as with a familiar Friend, and which finds harmony and peace by falling naturally into step with the purposes of Providence. The twice-born type is aware of disunity, division, a rift at the centre of being, something in oneself that is out of gear and out of step and needs righting. St. Paul is the great type of it, and the heart of the need for second birth is his cry: " Wretched man that I am! Who shall deliver me from the body of this death? " The once-born type takes naturally to goodness and elevated activity which makes for happiness and peace. The twice-born type is beset with anxieties and inward friction which can only find happy activity after an inward readjustment has taken place.

A great many of us belong to the twice-born group, or ought to belong to it, who need to find it out. We like to think we are once-born, and all right as we are. We have glossed over the division and disunity within us by a fictitious outward self-possession and quietness. But the rift can only be fully healed when we have given ourselves over to God.

Now, for this twice-born type, there are two possible ways of surrendering. A surrender may be largely a deliberate act of will. A man having seen the issue of surrender, and knowing that God wants the whole of his life unreservedly, may make the plunge and throw himself utterly upon God to do with as He will. Such a surrender is that described in the *Life of Prof. Henry B. Wright*,[1] of Yale,

---

[1] By George Stewart, p. 18.

where he says, of a meeting he attended at North-field: " I was afraid I should be asked to go as a foreign missionary, but I went down. There, seated in an armchair at one end of the room, was the greatest human I have ever known, Dwight L. Moody. He spoke to us simply and briefly about the issues of life, using John 7:17 as his theme: ' If any man willeth to do his will, he shall know of the teaching, whether it be of God, or whether I speak from myself.' There in the quiet, without anyone knowing what was going on, I gave myself to God, my whole mind, heart and body: and I meant it." Those of you who know of Henry Wright's profound influence for more than twenty years upon student life in this country, and the emphasis he always put on the need for absolute surrender to God's will, will not ask whether such an experience is lasting; you will know that it is both lasting and widely multiplying.

I could give you a hundred instances of men and women whom I have known, who have, at a critical place in their lives, made this momentous turning and have never retraced their steps or gone back on their decision. You may be the kind of person who, having seen the choice, must deliberately, coolly, sanely and with resolve, hand yourself to God by making a deed of trust for your life, disposing of yourself to Him so that you can never take yourself back again.

There are others of this twice-born type who cannot thus take the kingdom of heaven by force. There are two elements in the complete experience of which I speak, if surrender grows into conversion: man's turn, and God's search. For some of us, the critical element is the dedication of our own wills. For others it is the moment of God's invasion. Surrender is, then, not so much effort as is required in throwing ourselves over upon the mercy of God, but only so much effort as is needed to open the door of our life to Him. We must all know that what God does for us in a conversion is the great matter, and not what we do for ourselves: but there are natures in which this is the supreme part, in the sense that surrender is a passive thing rather than an active one. I am not now talking about resignation under pain and trouble, which is quite another question. I am speaking of the need for an open and relaxed and unstruggling mind as the medium through which God can alone come into the lives of some people. Possibly there is an element of each emphasis needed in us all, so that we both make the effort of deliberate self-surrender and also cease from all effort, so that no exertion on our part may interfere with God's dealing with us. We may not be able to tell which is to be our particular means of surrendering, until we try it.

One is bound to be asked the question whether this is a sudden or a gradual matter. I believe that it is a relatively sudden matter for many, and a combination of suddenness and gradualness for others. For the person who wakes up to the fact that they are matured in every other way, but babes in their spiritual development, so that the great experience of religion has yet to come, I believe that it is likely to be an experience which takes place at a definite and recognized time. It is significant that

James wrote: " Self-surrender has been and always must be regarded as the vital turning-point of the religious life. . . . One may say that the development of Christianity in inwardness has consisted in little more than the greater and greater emphasis attached to this crisis of self-surrender." Crisis, mark you, not process.

The process which comes before the act of surrender is the long discovery that the way of self is no way at all, and leads nowhither—the lonely, despairing, feverish desire to be rid of oneself. And the process which comes after the act of surrender is the steady matching-up of the actual with the ideal, the rethinking and remoulding life in accordance with the great decision. Both processes may take time, much time. But the decision itself has the definiteness about it which any decision has: you may prepare long for a decision, you may work long to carry it out. But when you decide, the hammer falls, and there cannot be delay.

Now I want to speak of four immediate results of surrender, when one has wholly let go of one's life, and is living continually with reference to God. By these I think it fair to test whether we have surrendered or not.

The first is a wide sense of liberation. The queer thing about self-will is that it kills the very thing it wants, freedom. If you know any more abject slave than the man or woman who has throughout his life had his own way, I would like to know where you find one. One of my friends tells me, when I talk to him along these lines: " I feel as if you were trying to put a big, black overcoat on me, and button it tight." But it is precisely his own complete control of the issues of his life which is, year after year, buttoning the overcoat tighter and tighter; and it is the very surrender which he fears that alone can bring him liberty. There is no freedom under God's wide heaven like the freedom of having committed yourself, lock, stock and barrel, to the will of God. The joy of it is an unearthly thing, which follows you and grows greater with the years.

The next result is an inquiry into one's life-plans in the large, to see if they be such as God would choose as His first, best plan for us. For younger people this is bound to concern their life-work and their marriage, and to demand that these great choices be made upon a basis of honest search for God's will. There are in the world a great many empty places, hard places, thrilling places which the world cannot see as thrilling. God wants workers there. There is a lot He wants done in this world, and there are very few who will lay themselves open to His plan, and promise to fit in wherever He says. Here, again, many a man or woman fears he must become a missionary, or give up what promises to be a successful worldly marriage to wait for one with better foundations; and it seems a heavy cross. Yet when one makes the commitment with regard to these larger life-plans, he finds that God makes no mistakes, and the thing he thought he could never do may be the very thing he loves to do most.

There is a retroactive element in a genuine surrender, too. You cannot give your life to God without being willing to turn back into the past, and there make right the things you know to have been wrong. Past wrong leaves its roots in our subconscious minds, and if you dig below the soil you will find the old foundations just as they were left. Personal relationships which have been filled with misunderstandings and irritation, business deals which have compromised with principle, injustice which calls for the fairness to reopen the question, rudeness or criticism or tale-bearing which only honest apology and confession will make right—these things feel the change in the atmosphere when we have genuinely surrendered, and they must be acclimatized to the new life. Nobody has really given in to God who leaves untouched the unforgiven grudge, or the unrighted wrong. The new life demands a clean slate.

And then there must be growing victory over sin. Deliverance!—that was the cry of victory of Christianity to the first century. St. Paul went into a rotten port-city like Corinth, infested with all the degradation of the worst of Greek degeneracy, and told his people he was determined to know nothing among them but Jesus Christ. Real Christianity has always been able to save men from sin. And when I find people who have all their lives been coming to church, and have never mastered a quick tongue, a disagreeable spirit, the touchiness which resents the slightest interference with one's own desires, and which makes one hard to get along with, I do not say that Christianity has failed, I say that we Christians have simply not surrendered our whole hearts to the Lord Jesus Christ.

For two nights of this past week my work has carried me to the Jerry McAuley Water Street Mission.[1] I heard there the vivid and simple and unostentatious testimonies of men who had been redeemed from all kinds of sin. They said they had been kept for two days, several weeks, twenty years, by the power of Christ. There is a difference between that happy and vivid and unashamed religion, and our decent and reticent and less effective kind: the difference isn't in the amount of decency nearly so much as it is in the amount of power. I would to God the churches of this city had in them the power that is there, that we expected people to be converted as they do, expected them to witness as they do. And back of that power over broken sin there lies a great yielding, a deep surrender to the love and will of God.

Now, my friends, I always want to say a special word in a sermon like this to those whose major choices seem to have been made, and who feel it is now a question of making the best of it because it is too late to change. It is never too late. When you miss God's first best plan for you, He has a second, and if you miss that, a third. Your situation is always new to God. He can and will always begin over again to deal with you, and give you another chance. It is a great thing to surrender to God in the fulness of youth, but it is also a great thing to surrender at any time. I beg you not to think of yourselves as too far along the way to change.

---

[1] Since this was written, Calvary Church has opened its own Rescue Mission at 346 East Twenty-third Street, New York City.

Let us to-day ask ourselves with complete can-
dour whether we ever have surrendered everything
to His will. Did we miss His whole plan for us
years ago by taking a turn we knew was wrong?

Have we felt the pressure of His love all these
years, and feared to respond to it, as Francis
Thompson did, " lest having Him, I should have
naught beside "?

Have we let sin creep in somewhere till we take
it for part of us which we cannot strip away and
get free from?

Have we given Him our homes, our money, our
ambition, our joy, our suffering, our human ties,
our characters, our hearts? Is there somewhere a
conscious withholding?—for if there is, there is so
much less of that freedom and joy and peace in
believing which comes alone when we give all.

It is one of the dearest hopes of my life that this
congregation will learn the art of winning lives to
Jesus Christ: the beginning is with ourselves. No
man can give what he does not possess. You cannot ask another to give himself to Christ till you
have given yourself. This is no academic self-
examination. Something is desperately wrong with
our modern version of Christianity, and I suspect
that it is the want of just this surrender amongst us.
I believe you are in or out. Henry Wright startled
some people once by saying: " No man or woman
oozes unconsciously into the kingdom of God. In
the final analysis, all enlist, and every soldier knows
when he enlisted." But I believe he was right.
Have you ever enlisted? Or have you all your life
hung around the recruiting station, and thought

about it? God has a place for you, a work for you to do. You will do it, or it will go undone.

" Who then offereth willingly to consecrate himself this day unto Jehovah? "

Let us pray:

O God our Father, it is so easy for us to drift along, and say our prayers and sing our worship as though with all our hearts we loved to do Thy will. Thou knowest us better than we know ourselves, and in Thy presence we see how much of our life is outside Thy control. Grant us grace to give Thee everything we have and are, and use us for Thy glory. For the sake of Jesus Christ our Lord. Amen.

V

HOW TO KNOW THE WILL OF GOD

THIRTY-FIVE years ago a lithe and well-dressed Scotsman of middle age was visiting American universities and conferences. He was making public addresses and holding private interviews everywhere he went. He was a scientist of considerable reputation, and he was one of the first men to see his way through the problem of adopting a modern viewpoint towards history and science, while he kept hold of a vital and personal evangelical Christianity. That man's name was Henry Drummond. They were widely different, but he was a close and understanding friend of D. L. Moody's, and they worked together here, as they had worked together in England when Mr. Moody had been there years before.

Henry Drummond was a marvellous combination of analyst and partisan, scientist and enthusiast, investigator and propagandist. To many men is it given to be onlookers of life, who dissect it and anatomize it. And to many more is it given to throw themselves headlong into the thick of life as participants. But Henry Drummond mixed those two elements in his personality in such a way as to make him of peculiar service to our generation. He was possessed of a wide knowledge of science, and he loved the search for truth in scientific regions. But he loved men as well as truth; and the passion of his life was the winning of young men for Christ. He knew intimately well the hearts of thousands of men. I do not much listen to the pronouncements of men whose minds smell of books, when they come to practical matters of religion; for I do not trust them unless they also know life. Henry Drummond knew life, and lived it richly.

Now, anyone who knows much about people spiritually comes to feel, sooner or later, that the greatest problem any of us face is the problem of what we shall do about the will of God. When we come to believe in God at all, we come to believe in Him as having something definite to say about our lives. To believe in the fact of the will of God is only to believe in God in the concrete. As you cannot pray without words, so you cannot imagine God apart from His desires which touch us. There is at the heart of religion this marriage between the mystical and the moral. And Henry Drummond, with inerrant insight, went often into this great problem. It was the love of his life to do the will of God. He was no glib and facile interpreter of what it was: he spent long hours searching his Bible for light on the question. And when he had finished his study, this scholar seeking a truth of metaphysics, this devoted Christian trying to know the heart and mind of his God, he wrote down in the fly-leaf of his Bible these eight points:

1. Pray.
2. Think.
3. Talk to wise people, but do not regard their decision as final.
4. Beware of the bias of your own will, but do not be too much afraid of it (God never unnecessarily thwarts a man's nature and likings, and it is a mistake to think that His will is in the line of the disagreeable).
5. Meantime, do the next thing, for doing God's will in small things is the best preparation for knowing it in great things.
6. When decision and action are necessary, go ahead.
7. Never reconsider your decision when it is finally acted upon; and—
8. You will probably not find out till afterwards, perhaps long afterwards, that you were led at all.

Now, let me take these steps one at a time, and embroider them a little in detail, reminding you first that I am not sure I have in everything caught the sense of Henry Drummond, and that I am packing my own meaning into his phrases.

1. " Pray." It is a common thing to run to God in petulant and frantic demand, asking Him to tell us what to do. This may be the sudden reversal of a life of self-seeking and self-guidance; and it is not to be wondered at if not much guidance comes from Him. What we often seek is His approval, not His will. When we come in a great honesty, having put our own wills behind us, seeking candidly the mind of the Lord, it is generally rather plain sailing: a mood or disposition comes upon us

with light in it, or a direct thought flits across our mind with illumination. These experiences are too common amongst Christians for any of you to pooh-pooh them until you have tried honestly. But when we come only in curiosity, merely wondering what God might like us to do, quite different is the result. We get nowhere, prayer is a fog, we get up anxious and fretful and in a stew. To find God's will in prayer demands a colossal honesty in our minds. A man recently disputed my use of the word honesty in this connection: he said willingness and unselfishness I might use, but honesty implied dishonesty in coming to God with our minds made up. Yet this is precisely what we are; we are dishonest when we prejudice the will of God by trying to twist it into our own will: we are not honest with facts, especially the great fact that God's plan may not be our plan. " My thoughts are not your thoughts " is true more often than we care to remember. So that to pray for God's will to be revealed we must be ready and willing to have it revealed, and come to Him with an open mind.

There is in the city of New York the president of a great company. He is a devoted Christian, and it has been his practise to bring up his sons to attend church regularly on Sunday mornings till they are twenty-one; after that they are free to choose for themselves. One Sunday one of his sons came to him and said: " Father, there is a house party over in ——— to-day, and if you don't mind I shall take the car and go over." The father said: " Yes, son, you can go, under one condition." " What is that? " the son asked. " That you will go up-stairs and talk to God about it for fifteen minutes." And the son said: "Well, dad, I guess I won't go." That boy had learned already that in the realized presence of God, one sees things as they really are, if one is only honest and willing to see them.

Yet I recall a friend of mine speaking of his desire to know what he ought to do with his life. I asked if he had prayed about it. He said that he had, and he asked God what to do: but that if God had said certain things, he would not have been willing to do them. That is not prayer: it is a kind of blasphemy instead. It points the truth that no man can see the will of God who is not willing to see it. One of Drummond's favourite verses in this connection was John 7:17: " If any man *willeth* to do his will, he shall know." And wrapped up in that little verse there lies more empirical spiritual experience than almost anywhere else I know. This, then, is the first guide—to pray.

2. " Think." There is a moral obligation to be as intelligent as you can. Turn over the possibilities in your mind. Face all the facts you can find, honestly and fearlessly, I am not afraid of too much thought in religion, I am only afraid of too little of it. It is not sound reasoning which steals men's religion, it is half-baked rationalizing. Some people use their brains to convince themselves they ought to do what they want to do. Jesus says, against this kind of thing: " Judge not according to appearance, but judge righteous judgment." It may be a good thing to put down the pros and cons in two written columns, and weigh one against the other. If the decision concerns your life-work, face the

needs of the world frankly, as well as your own qualifications. We are apt to be too subjective in some of these questions. I believe we do well to look out on the world, and ask what it is which that world needs most, and then ask ourselves how we can best supply that need—rather than to turn in upon ourselves and ask what riches and talents lie hidden within us which we must find a way to turn loose upon the world. Look out, and assemble all the facts you can. There is nothing the matter with using human brains, so long as an honest character lies behind them. But this is an age of more self-deception, under the guise of intellectual honesty, than any I know about. Remember that, when all is said and done, God may communicate His wish to you, and knock your thinking endwise. To be thoroughgoingly, intellectually honest, you will consider as the greatest factor of all the will of God.

3. " Talk to wise people, but do not regard their decision as final." That is, don't expect them to make up your mind for you. Consult them for what they are worth. But make the decision your own. There are always a lot of people in the world who like to talk to ministers, as if we knew it all: they run to us to settle things they ought to be close enough to God to settle for themselves. And we are always in danger of priding ourselves upon our influence, and handing out packages of advice, when as a matter of fact we ought to be dealing with a larger issue, the issue of their surrender to God's will, and their own search for what it is. Now, don't discuss this with just anybody you happen to think about, but with people who love God and His

will and are themselves putting the kingdom of
heaven first.

A friend of mine went to a business man in Phila-
delphia who had asked him to come into business
with him: and when he told him he had decided for
the ministry, and asked what he thought of it, the
business man said: " You d——— f———." Now,
a man like that forfeits his right ever to advise anybody. A man who will drench a young man's aspirations with that kind of materialistic cold water is
not fit to make suggestions to a pig. Go to really
wise people, wise with God's wisdom: and He will
often speak to you through them, as generally He
does speak through others. But let this talk be for
a *clearing* of the issue, not for a *settlement* of it.
What they say to you is valid only insofar as it
rings a bell in your own heart.

4. " Beware of the bias of your own will, but do
not be too much afraid of it (God never unnecessarily thwarts a man's nature and likings, and it is
a mistake to think that His will is in the line of the
disagreeable)." Drummond was talking to Scots-
men with consciences a yard long when he added to
his universal warning: " Beware of the bias of your
own will," the balance, " But do not be too much
afraid of it." I think the first half of it is probably
more applicable to us. We are not likely to err
on the side of interpreting God's will hardly, but
softly. When you consult God and your mind is
already partially made up, you need very seriously
to beware of that bias, for it will throw out all the
calculations. Left to ourselves, we are very likely
to please ourselves.

And yet we need the postscript, too: " Do not be too much afraid of it. God never unnecessarily thwarts a man's nature and likings, and it is a mistake to think that His will is in the line of the disagreeable." It is a mistake, and a great one. I heard a woman say within a week that whatever was the hardest thing to do was probably God's will: but I do not believe that. Some people think God goes around hunting up hard and unhappy jobs, and then trailing them down and loading the jobs off on them. To make God that kind of a supernatural taskmaster is to be unchristian in our thought of Him. There are hard jobs to be done, and somebody has got to do them. But I feel sure that God made us for a particular piece of work, and that we shall never be fully happy until we find that work. You may not think it looks like you would enjoy it: but if it is His place you will, and you will never really be happy anywhere else.

5. " Meantime, do the next thing, for doing God's will in small things is the best preparation for knowing it in great things." Some are so preoccupied with the obvious that they never get above it to take a look at the whole: but some also are so busy with the abstract they never see the concrete, nor complete the ordinary duty which stares them in the face. A man who is honestly living up to the light he has, to-day, will have more light to-morrow, when he needs it. Sometimes God makes us wait for the full emergence of His plan. If we have been faithful in a few things, He will make us master of many things, revealing as much truth as we can live up to. I know a man in business in downtown New

York. He has been soundly changed in his own life, and he loves to bring Christ into the lives of men. He does not know whether God wants him to go into the ministry or not. Meanwhile he is doing a fine job in an insurance office, and working there until or unless he is guided to go elsewhere. There is an enormous amount of common sense about real religion which we miss sometimes because it is not exactly the common sense of the world at large.

6. " When decision and action are necessary, go ahead." Go ahead fearlessly. God will give you for each step as much light as you really need, and perhaps no more. You may see from here to the next corner, and there the path seems to turn down into the dark. Go that far, and more light will come. Do not wait till you see light on all the road before you: most of us never do see it. The Greeks used to wear lanterns on their shoes: it would throw light about three feet ahead of them, and then they had to take one more step to get three feet more of light. So it is with finding the will of God. You may not see all the sides of a question of importance, yet you must decide it. God will give you *enough* light. Do not rush Him, or the situation; but when you must, let the hammer fall, act on all the light you have, and you will make no mistake. The more you trust God in critical situations, the more you will learn that you can trust Him: and that if you will throw the onus of decision off yourself and on to Him, giving Him only a ready and obedient will, you will be amazed at the way things work out for you.

7. " Never reconsider the decision when it is

finally acted upon." That is of immense importance. Every thoughtful person, every conscien-
tious person, wonders again and again about an old
decision; wants to go back and tear it up by the
roots and ask again why it was ever made. Some
people do that about marriage, many do it about
their life's work. They acted in all good faith at
the time: but later they question their own decision.
It is a fatal thing to do. Now, if the decision was
made selfishly, we may have to make the best of a
bad margin; remembering that God has always a
substitute will which goes into the game when the
first-string will is put out. But if they acted under
God so far as they understood, it was the best they
could do. If trial and difficulty has come since, that
was meant to have its place. We should spend our
lives on regrets, and many do so spend them, if we
spent much time reconsidering decisions that have
been already acted upon. *Until* a decision is acted
upon, reconsider as much as you like. But afterwards, go forward and banish fear.

8. "You will probably not find out till afterwards, perhaps long afterwards, that you were led
at all." I should not put so much of an interval as
Drummond implies; for I believe that we often
know we acted rightly by a very quick sense of
being right, and sometimes by the manifest out-
working of God's plan which shows itself quickly.
And yet there is an immense truth here. He is
talking about totals and broad outlines. And one
finds that the great compensation for the steady
fleeing-away of the years is a larger and longer look
at one's own life, and a clearer view of the path by

which he has come. One sees here just the right
person coming across one's path to point a truth, or
to enlarge a horizon. There we came across that
great book that turned us upward. In another
place a great sorrow made us tender and kinder.
And the map of the will of God is not the track of
a railway stretching away before us, but rather the
wake of a ship lying white behind us. We see best
how clear that path is as we look back upon it over
a long period of time. I ask you to-day to look
back across your own life—not somebody's else, for
we never know all the factors anywhere but in our
own—look at your own life, and see whether, if you
have acted according to your best, and interpreted
events with a will to find God's purpose, things
have not marvellously worked together for good.

But we end where we began. Prayer is the heart
of the discovery of the will of God. I will defend it
against all comers that something happens when a
man lays his life open before God, and asks Him to
make known His will, which cannot happen by any
amount of uninspired thought or human direction.
We see into the heart of things in prayer like that.
But that kind of prayer is impossible without rad-
ical and basic surrender to the will of God first.
" If any man willeth to do his will "—this means,
no grudging concession to God, but whole-hearted
allegiance and the co-operation of one's whole self
—" he shall know." The man who knows God's
will is the man who loves it. The man who finds
out what God wants is the man who cares what God
wants, who feels upon him the same kind of bur-
dens God feels and carries. If God can count on

you, He can commit His secrets to you. We have got to get on God's side before it's any use to ask what is God's plan.

As Drummond finished his address in Appleton Chapel, at Harvard, thirty-five years ago, he said: "Above all things, do not touch Christianity unless you are willing to seek the kingdom of God first. I promise you a miserable existence if you seek it second." That is true. And the matter with many who call themselves Christians, and have never found any thrill and power in their religion, lies just there: they are not seeking the kingdom first.

But when you do come out on that side with all your heart, and seek the kingdom first, I can promise you not a miserable existence, but the only thing that satisfies on this side of eternity. I say to you that it will be the tragedy of your life to miss the will of God, and the standing and crowning success of your life to find it. There is no other success than to do what God wants you to do.

"Not every one that saith unto me, Lord, Lord, shall enter into the kingdom of heaven; but he that doeth the will of my Father who is in heaven."

God give us the grace to ask: "Lord, what wilt thou have me to do?"

Let us pray:

O God, who in Thy love for us dost plan for us a way far better than our own: Grant us to desire Thy will above all things, and desiring it, to seek it; and seeking it, to find it; and finding it, to serve Thee faithfully and to make Thee known to men. Through Jesus Christ our Lord.

VI

THE FELLOWSHIP OF THE HOLY GHOST

". . . The fellowship of the Holy Ghost."
—II Corinthians 13:14.

THIS is Whitsunday. The derivation is apparently from White-Sunday, the day when the catechumens were dressed in white for confirmation, a custom begun some time during the Middle Ages. It is the Church's yearly memorial of the great event of Pentecost, when the disciples were gathered " with one accord in one place," and the Holy Spirit came upon them.

There are many thoughts which stir in one's mind when one comes to this great day of Pentecost, about which one would like to have the time to preach. There is that in a genuine experience of the Holy Spirit which would solve a great many of our typical problems and our tragic ills. It would solve the problem of " spiritualism " which seeks, by an unauthentic route, to find contact with the other world: it would do away with the uncertainty which is poisoning so much of modern life: it might even cure our inflated intellectualism by the manifestation of a greater wisdom than this world can offer.

But I have chosen one thought, one very great thought, connected with the Pentecost experience:

66

and that is " the fellowship of the Holy Ghost."
You all recognize it as a phrase from our most
familiar benediction, which closes the Second Epis-
tle to the Corinthians.

I have generally understood that phrase, I suspect in company with most of you, to mean something which I find a closer study discards. I have
been accustomed to think that the beloved benediction which begins " The grace of our Lord Jesus
Christ. . .," prays for a special attachment on our
part to each Person of the Trinity—so that " the
fellowship of the Holy Ghost " would mean " the
companionship of the Holy Ghost " severally in our
own hearts.

This is probably a false interpretation. The
phrase refers to something which seems to have
been a very definite apostolic concept; namely, the
fellowship of believing people which was created by
the Holy Ghost, rather than fellowship individually
with the Holy Ghost Himself. You will readily see
that these are two very different ideas: one is an individual, the other is a corporate experience. One
finds the Holy Spirit unmediated: the other finds
Him through the group-experience of men and
women like-minded.

Now, when one leaves behind the immediate results of the coming of the Spirit at Pentecost, this
fellowship is the great residuum. We all remember
the tongues of fire, and the speaking with tongues,
and St. Peter's interpretation of what happened as
the fulfilment of God's promise to pour out His
Spirit upon all flesh—the way the crowd who heard
him were convicted and subsequently baptized into

the Church. Those were the mode of the experience: but the thing which was left was what they called " the Fellowship." There is a verse later in the same account which says: " They continued steadfastly in the apostles' teaching, and fellowship, in the breaking of bread and the prayers." But in the Greek there is an article before the word for fellowship, *koinonia*, which makes the phrase an independent one, as most modern commentators recognize. It was not just " fellowship," it was a particular one, " *the* fellowship." It means they continued, not in the apostles' teaching and fellowship, but in the apostles' teaching, and the fellowship.

This was a new thing. And to it was given its distinctive name. As this word for fellowship is used through the Acts and the Epistles, it makes us feel that it is not a common word in its common usage, it is a common word lifted from common usage into special. They looked for some language of earth in which to express a heavenly experience of being spiritually welded, as they found they were by Pentecost. This was not, mark you again, merely a fellowship of the believers amongst themselves, nor yet a fellowship of men and women each of whom was linked individually with the Holy Spirit: it is the much profounder experience of fellowship between those who had found the Holy Spirit together, and were still understanding Him with a corporate understanding. It was such an experience as made them aware of the third side of the triangle in every relationship which they had. When they were with another believer they were experiencing his experience of the Holy Spirit—when they were individually linked with the Holy Spirit, in prayer and inspiration, they were bound to recognize that they first knew Him through the body of other believers. This was, I say, a wholly new thing, requiring a new name, " The Fellowship "—and as I study it, it seems to me perhaps the most significant bearing which Pentecost has upon the life of the Church to-day. It preceded and moulded the " organization " of the Church—it was the vital spiritually creative urge which later took the form of the organized " ecclesia."

The symbol of that fellowship was the broken loaf, or bread, as we translate it. In the verse where we read of the after-life of those Pentecost-converts: " They continued in the apostles' teaching, and the fellowship, and the breaking of bread, and the prayers." There seems to have been more symbolic meaning attached to the breaking of the bread, to its brokenness, than came later to be the case. And it stood, not only for the broken body of Christ, but also for the body of believers, broken, as they were, through giving up their own wills for Christ's, broken by persecution also, and then the mingled particles kneaded into one Christian body.

The outward character of the fellowship was actual brotherhood and " togetherness " of the very most profound and intense kind. We read that " all that believed were together." It was as though a corporate personality had been developed, a group becoming almost a spiritual individual, thinking and experiencing and understanding together. We read also that they " had all things common: and they sold their possessions and goods, and parted them to all, according as any man had need." It is too absurd for denial to call this, as it frequently has been called, " an experiment in communism ": they cared nothing for the economics of the matter, it was a spontaneous expression of spiritual fellowship, equalizing the material inequalities of the believers, and giving simply because a spiritual brother had need. Ananias' sin of withholding was not only the sin of falsehood, but the sin of reason and disloyalty.

The pledge to the outside world of the reality of this fellowship was in its ethical results. To the believers were given exceptional and miraculous powers for the lifting and strengthening of life: there were the gifts of tongues, breaking down walls between differing nationalities, and obscure men found themselves integral parts of a movement tremendous with meaning, so that one lofty purpose held them continuously. The great word for the centre of the fellowship was *agape,* love: and this was no sentimental and effusive matter, it was genuine understanding and self-giving so great that all barriers went down before it, even the age-old barrier between Jew and Gentile. There is sarcasm when we say to-day: " See how these Christians love one another! "—but it was sober fact then. And with this went the quieter powers for living all of life with sweetness and kindness of spirit—what St. Paul called " the fruit of the Spirit, love, joy, peace, longsuffering, kindness, goodness, faithfulness, meekness, self-control." This was not the cooling-down of great powers to small, that men

who had had part in miracles became interested in
the gentle art of getting along with other people;
but rather the permeation by religion of the whole
of life—its long quiet stretches as well as its high
moments and crises.

But I believe that neither complete community of
thought and possession, nor elevation of moral life,
can account for the amazing effect of this fellowship
upon the world. There is a deeper cause. And it
lies in the common discovery of spiritual truth, the
insight which came from " the fellowship of the
Holy Ghost." There is about the apostolic company of disciples an unmistakable mark of sheer
vitality, of heightened powers and amplified possibilities which means they have struck a whole new
vein of truth about life. What St. Paul called *epig-
nosis*, knowledge, was far beyond anything we find
in ordinary education, or any collection of facts,
or any human body of truth: it was the window
into ultimate reality, the knowledge of this world
which comes from being closely acquainted with
the other.

Consider what it did for those who set down our
Gospels and Epistles, the most immortal literature
of the ages, coming forth from the minds of simple
men, " trailing clouds of glory " because they had
been touched with the inspiration of the Holy
Spirit. Consider the effect upon the mind of St.
Paul: admittedly he would have been a great mind
anyway, he was thus endowed. But under the
dominance of the Spirit he became more than the
philosopher he would have been in any case, more
than sage or poet, he became seer and prophet, re-

vealer of the hidden things of God, so that we forget the gigantic intellectual faculties of St. Paul in wonder at the contemplation of his spiritual intuition. All this literary output came forth through the experiences of the fellowship: they shared often in its writing and composition, they shared always in the life out of which it was produced.

But there is a still more remarkable phase of spiritual understanding than the heightening of what we should call intellectual faculties. I mean the group-experience of being led by the Holy Spirit, both in their own daily walk and conversation, and particularly in their conquest of the world about them. Not only were they set apart from the paganism round about by purity and elevation of life, but they became ingenious in their witness to that same paganism, and turned it by hundreds into their own fellowship. This implies a sure-footedness, a continuous inspiration, a group-guidance which was the great effective element in the beginnings of Christianity. They were melted down into such a spiritual unity amongst themselves, born of love and of honesty and of spiritual fellowship, that they stood and thought and attacked like one living individual.

This was not conformity and imitation; it was the highest form of individualism and liberty, the liberty which has learned perfect loyalty. The Spirit can communicate His truth to a spiritual fellowship of believers in ways He cannot communicate it to individuals: it is another phase of Christ's meaning when He said that " where two or three are gathered together in my name, there am I in the midst of them." He is wherever a believer is: but He is present in heightened reality in the fellowship. And His will is clarified by the corrective and perspective which one derives from the experience, not of general humanity, but of his brothers in the faith. This was what bound into unbreakable unity the disciples of the early Church, and what made the early Church the superb and supreme example in all history of what a little group of entirely consecrated and indivisibly united people can do against the world.

You will not have followed me thus far without realizing that I have much more in mind than a historic study of one result of Pentecost. You have been all along conscious of how far our own church, and our contemporaneous Christianity, falls short of even a parallel or analogous experience to this which we have been considering. Pentecost was not an isolated event: soon after it there followed another time when the disciples were praying for strength to withstand their persecutors and to witness bravely, and " the place was shaken wherein they were gathered together; and they were all filled with the Holy Spirit, and they spake the word of God with boldness." And down through the history of the Church there have been many times when a group of believers stepped out boldly upon God's promises, dared to take Him at His word, dared to break with the world and then turn round to capture it for Christ: and to them the daring Spirit of God could entrust Himself with special revealing and guiding power, making of the group of believers a channel of God into the world, the

pattern of a new order of social relationships, and
a phalanx almost military in unity and power, for
conquest of the world without. There have been
repetitions of Pentecost. Great spiritual move-
ments, gathering about such names as Francis and
Tauler and Wesley and Loyola, have always been
group-movements.

Is it day-dreaming to believe that such a movement might come in our time, in our world? God
does not give Himself by accident. There is always
a time of testing, and proof of dependability; then
comes the great revelation. There was a moral and
a spiritual basis for Pentecost: it came to discip-
lined, dedicated, self-forgetful lives, centred in
Jesus Christ as Lord and Saviour, as Master and
Friend. It came when they needed it, and when
they were gathered together for inner strengthening, to do their great work in the world of standing
for the Gospel and spreading it. If God found a
group of us, each committed beyond recall in his
own soul to Jesus Christ, paying the price of Christian fellowship one with another, burdened to make
Christ effective in New York as He began to be
effective in Jerusalem—forgetting our conventional
little fears and hesitancies—leaving behind us the
icy formality of our religion which extends even
towards those who come with us into God's house,
seeking this same supreme thing as we ourselves—a
group made up of every human type differing in the
outward things of taste and talent, but all the more
united because superficial dissimilarities were forgotten through the one great possession of Christ—
God might again break through, and astonish the

world through a brotherhood of His transfigured lives.

Dead Christians and half-dead Christians short-circuit that kind of power. There are groups of nominal Christian people amongst whom Pentecost is forever out of the question. I suspect prosperity is inimical to it in a church, I know that complacency and coldness of spirit are. There is not even common, human friendliness in some churches: how can there ever be spiritual fellowship? And there are other churches where all direct action of the Spirit of God upon human souls is explained away by natural and psychological processes: you will not find Pentecost repeated where men no longer believe in Pentecost, but name it some variety of social emotion.

But the field is whitening to a harvest. New York needs Pentecost. A young business man of wealth and culture, with all that belongs to this world and little that belongs to the other, said to me this week: " Don't you think the time is ripe for a big evangelistic push right here in New York? " It was a significant and revealing question from that kind of a man. I believe he spoke for thousands who want an authentic reinterpretation of Gospel and apostolic Christianity to-day. There are sections of New York that *want* Pentecost. They are not the conventionally religious sections. If one church found " the fellowship of the Holy Ghost," and let loose through this city a group of inspired individuals with a message from on high—and one day that group were found " with one accord in one place," coming together for fresh fire, for more life, thrust together by the persecution of one part of the world without, and by the spiritual hunger of the other part, bound to one another in this closest of all ties—God might choose so to manifest Himself again to men.

Let us search our hearts for what in us would hinder such an event from taking place right here. Let us be conscious again of our weakness by ourselves. And then let us dare to look up into the face of God, and pray with humility and with boldness:

" Come, Holy Ghost, *our* souls inspire."

In the stillness, let us pray to the Lord of Pentecost.

Silent Prayer.

O Holy Ghost, Lord and Giver of Life: Grant unto the Church such fellowship through Thee as made her powerful and invincible at the beginning. Come again with great might into our midst, and fill us with the fire of cleansing and illumination: and send us forth aflame with Thee into the world. Through Jesus Christ our Lord. Amen.

VII

THE IMPORTANCE OF INDIVIDUALS

"Jesus saw Nathanael . . ."—John 1:47.

JESUS had been talking with a new disciple, named Philip. In the brief period of his discipleship, Philip had caught the infection with which Jesus filled His followers, the redemptive infection, the passion to bring men to God. And, moving off from Jesus a little, Philip spoke to a friend of his named Nathanael. Philip made a great announcement to him. He said that the great expectation of Moses and the prophets was here, Jesus of Nazareth. And as they talked together, reasoning whether the Messiah should spring from so unlikely a village as Nazareth, they were moving towards Jesus.

Jesus stood watching this action—watching it, I suspect, with the most tremendous kind of excitement, and the profoundest kind of joy, that ever gladdened His heart while He lived in our world. To see another take fire at one's own highest enthusiasm is joy beyond joy. He was taking it all in, missing nothing of its import and incident. He called Nathanael by name, greatly to his surprise; and then He complimented the spiritual sincerity of his life. Nathanael was astonished: " Whence knowest thou me? " And Jesus told him that He had seen him under the fig tree, before Philip called him. The amazed man said: " Rabbi, thou art the Son of God; thou art the King of Israel! " And Jesus said: " Do you believe in me just because I saw you under the fig tree? You will see greater things than that! "

I want to ask you to attempt to understand something of the consciousness of a Man who, while talking with a friend, was also taking in a stranger—seeing in the friend a roadway into the life of the stranger—studying the posture, the face, the probable tastes, the aspirations of the stranger, whom most men would have missed by the roadside as he sat under a fig tree. There was in Jesus such a preoccupation with individuals, such a knowledge of " what was in man," as I think never anywhere else existed on this planet.

When Jesus " saw " Nathanael, much more was involved than being aware of a man moving towards Him. This was not only eyesight: it was insight. He not only beheld the presence of a man, but He saw through into the heart and meaning of that man. He took in Nathanael's spirituality of nature, calling him " an Israelite indeed, in whom is no guile "—a sincere man, that is; not a sinless man, but a man in spiritual earnest—one of those whose faith He came " not to destroy but to fulfil." Probably Nathanael was one of those spiritually refined and reticent people who must be carefully drawn out by sympathy, or they will close up entirely. This word of commendation was like a warm sun to draw a bud into bloom. Jesus understood much more about Nathanael than Nathanael was aware of. He " saw " his sincerity, his aspiration, his shyness perhaps, his spiritual hunger, perhaps his need, though He said nothing of it so early in the conversation. Next time you " see " somebody, ask yourself whether you " see " them with any vestige of the comprehension with which Jesus saw Nathanael.

And He says that He was watching him before Philip called him, while he was under the fig tree. What was happening while he was under the fig tree? He may have closed his eyes in prayer, and Jesus saw that. He may have had on his face the strain and anguish of temptation, and Jesus saw that. He may have been looking off into the heavens, waiting for Messiah in company with that devout segment of Judaism which waited for Him, and Jesus saw that. Nathanael under the fig tree. Jesus had nothing else and nothing more to go on. Yet He read that hint as though it had been an exposition. From that detail He built up a careful analysis of a man. It led to Nathanael's discipleship. He is an obscure person, never again mentioned in the gospels, until he stands by the lakeside in the dawn of a morning after the resurrection, where Jesus reveals Himself. But the fact is, Nathanael began his discipleship on the day when he was understood—understood by Jesus, who had a genius for understanding individuals.

One of the very greatest needs of our day is a reawakening of the consciousness of the individual. All through our life we need to learn the wonderful art of Jesus, the art of seeing people.

It is needed in business. We have heard a great

deal about welfare and safety devices in business—about better housing and recreational facilities and trained psychiatrists to watch the health of the workers. And it is all good, very good. Would God we had more of it, and every business were progressive enough to include it. But there is one danger in it all, the danger of doing all this simply to increase the efficiency of the men, simply to fill the coffers of the business. And there is another danger, that it may all be mass-welfare which forgets the individual. The business which sees men, not as economic units to be made efficient, but as human individualities and souls to be developed and enriched through their work—that is the only kind of business which can have Jesus' approval. And wherever any of us are employing people in order to grind out of them what we can, without concerning ourselves with their own highest and best life, we are so far not Christians at all. I heard a Christian business-woman this week tell of her firm voluntarily raising the pay to a truckman who was losing money at the rates he asked, but who had made no request of them whatever: and of paying for him a debt he had contracted. That kind of thing must be well-pleasing to our Father in heaven: and it makes for bonds of loyalty which strengthen all human efforts.

It is needed in medicine. I am sometimes frightened at the sheer magnitude of the schemes and the institutions we are making for the prevention and relief of human sickness. There is no more merciful, Christlike work in the world than the work of doctors and nurses: no more gloriously Christian

building on earth than a hospital. But I believe
the restoration of health has in it an infinite number of non-material factors—factors which can only
be dealt with by the most delicate impingement of
personality upon personality. We all know how
needed is confidence in the nurse and doctor, if a
patient is to recover to maximum. But there are
yet more spiritual factors necessary. A psychia-
trist said to me a few weeks ago that ninety per
cent of the people who came to him needed to have
restored their faith in the worthwhileness of living.
That is not a material matter, it is profoundly a
spiritual matter. No man can manage that in
crowds: it requires intimate, personal concern. It
was said that Dr. Osler could almost tell what a
man needed the moment he walked in the office.
God give us doctors who are spiritual diagnosticians
as well—and we shall scotch bad-health off the face
of the earth!

We need the consciousness of individuals in education. The tendency in education to-day seems to
be towards maximum scientific efficiency: and that
means the intellectual survival of the fittest. There
are hordes of college professors to-day who consider
that they have no responsibility whatever beyond
the transfer of certain collections of information
from their heads to the heads of their students. I
believe that real education means helping people to
find the best that has been thought and said in the
world, and then to act upon it. It is no easy thing
to get from twelve to twenty: and to be herded
according to mental tests, without regard for those
intricacies of personality which differentiate us one

from the other, produces disastrous moral and psychological results. I dare to say that the profoundest understanding of human beings is impossible except upon a basis of personal acquaintance and sympathy; and that without religion, and the peculiar insight into life which genuine religion brings, the highest kind of sympathy cannot be developed.

The story is told of an old professor at Princeton, many years ago, who learned from another student that something he had said in his philosophy lecture had upset the mind of one of his Freshmen. That evening this old man, whom I remember and who was very fat, went up five flights of stairs to the room of this Freshman, rapped at his door and went into his room, saying: " I understand something I said this morning bothered your faith: and I want to come round and talk about it." That Freshman is the Secretary for Home Missions in one of the great churches of this country. And he will never forget the reverence for his own soul of that professor of philosophy. God send us teachers like that!

But perhaps it comes back more to our churches than to anything else. Theoretically we stand for a consciousness of the individual, because theoretically we stand for Christ. Again and again, when I speak with Christians and Christian workers about work for individuals, they say to me: " Of course—that is what I have always emphasized. The individual is the only thing that matters." But, my friends, the most dangerous things for religion are always the things to which religion says:

" Of course." We have said, " Of course," to the
creeds, till the life has gone out of them. We have
said, " Of course," to making a more fraternal
world, till we no longer stop to ask whether we ourselves are brotherly. We have said, " Of course,"
to the Sermon on the Mount, till its terrible demands roll off us like so much water from a roof.
Sometimes I see a safe and complacent kind of
Christian carrying a Bible in his hand: and I wonder the dynamite in that old Book doesn't go off in
his hands, and blow his safety to pieces! That's
not a book for cautious and unadventurous people: it is the record of lives who, when they found
God, found themselves in conflict with most of
what the world about them stood for. Beware of
saying, " Of course," lest you should not mean
what you say!

I say that the Church of Christ needs an awakening of the consciousness of the individual. We
need a Church which " sees " people, as Jesus saw
Nathanael. It is possible to go to a great many
churches and never hear a word of welcome, nor
find the slightest opportunity for Christian friend-
ship. If we are to go further with " seeing " individuals, we must begin upon the simplest level of
common human friendliness. We've got to drop
the pious discourtesy inside God's house which has
driven so many from us forever.

But it goes deeper than this. We must gauge our
whole work for Christ to the needs of individuals,
as I believe He gauged His. Our organizations are,
on the whole, adapted for the group and not the
individual: we think more in terms of clubs and

committees than we do in terms of people. Our sermons are aimed at congregations, and they ought to be aimed at individual lives, at the problems and sorrows and interests which hold the attention of people individually. We ministers need much more definite training in dealing with individuals than we usually get in theological seminaries. I was with a group of twenty ministers recently, and I went round the circle asking how many of them, while in seminary, had had any real training in meeting the needs of individuals, in going out to capture unredeemed lives for Jesus Christ—and, of the lot, one man said that there was one hour in his three-year course when somebody had talked about work like that! That is a shame and a scandal, and you lay-people ought to rise up and demand something better—for your own spiritual lives suffer from the lack in your ministers.

It is a monstrous spectacle to see an average church, say, of two or three hundred people, with one minister expected single-handed to care for the spiritual life of those people; and yet forced to carry the thousand fretful details of administration and executive work, when he ought to be steeping his mind in good reading, and his soul in prayer and meditation, and his life in the common life of his people. My own situation is so happily different from this that I can speak about it for some of my brothers. But I think it is no wonder many a minister gives up hope of reaching many individuals and settles down to meeting you in the mass.

We need to expect a great deal more of our people in actual spiritual experience. I am sometimes

appalled at how little difference religion can make in a human life where, possibly for years, for half a lifetime, the formalities and outwardnesses of religion have been practiced: and yet the quality of that life—its timidity, its defeat, its moral mediocrity—has never been perceptibly changed. I say that no amount of organization can ever remedy things like that. The only cure there, is for a man of God, be he layman or minister, to begin to pray, and to go to that person willing to give, as St. Paul said, "Not the gospel of God only, but also our own souls," and lead that person into a profounder experience of God through Christ. We need a Church and a ministry that sees people "under the fig tree," in the time of crises, in the hour of need; sees them as they are, sees them also as they might be; turns the sceptic into the disciple, as Jesus and Philip turned Nathanael.

What might not come if a church should develop such a consciousness of the importance of the individual, that all its work, even its group-work, was arranged for the individual? Suppose some church began by being friendly and welcoming, and went on to train a group of people who could actually meet the needs of individuals, who knew how to carry unconvinced people into a genuine experience of Christ—so that a congregation became, not a lot of disjointed individuals, but a brotherhood shot through with human links—what might not that church do in a great city? Someone asked a friend of mine for his creed awhile ago, and he said: "People are more important than things, and God can guide."

I confess that my hopes for this parish Church of Calvary lie in this very direction. We are off the beaten track, thank God. People come to us because they want to, not because it is convenient or conventional. We are given the chance to do a qualitative as against a quantitative work, an individual as against a mass-work. I wish with all my heart that this might come to be known as the church of the individual, where we " see " people with a fragment of the same understanding with which Jesus " saw " Nathanael. The great Dr. Alexander Whyte, of Free St. George's, Edinburgh, was once called " a specialist in sin: " he profoundly understood the subtleties of sin, and its ravages in human personality. In the same spirit, I wish that this church might be known as a specialist in the individual, as a place where there is always time for everybody who wants help, where the importance of the individual is never forgotten, for the Lord Jesus Christ never forgot it.

Will you not, good Christian people, carry more of that spirit of the consciousness of individuality with you wherever you go? As I walked down the street one afternoon this week, I was aware that I " saw " almost nobody—*like* the blind man in the Bible, when he was only half-cured, they were " men as trees walking." That's not good enough. Let us pray for more of Christ's understanding and insight, just in our ordinary way of taking people day by day. Let us see spiritual possibilities where we saw only scepticism or indifference before, disciples in strangers. Let us pray that Christ will touch our eyes afresh, till as individuals and as a

church we " see every man clearly,"—and so fulfil
the law of the love of Christ.

Let us pray:
O God, our Father, who beholdest each one of us
as though we were an only child: Help us to look
upon others with the love wherewith Thou lookest
upon us. Grant to us something of the beautiful
sympathy and understanding of Christ. Keep us
from ever passing over anybody as though they did
not matter. Fill our churches and fill our hearts
with real love for people: and help us to serve them
and to reveal Thee to them. Through Jesus Christ
our Lord. Amen.

VIII

ISAIAH'S VISION OF GOD

" Here am I: send me."—Isaiah 6:8.

THIS is Trinity Sunday. It is ordinarily a time when we give ourselves to thinking about the nature of God. I am an ardent Trinitarian. I do not believe that the Trinity is a matter only of abstract metaphysical speculation: I believe that the doctrine grew out of authentic spiritual discoveries which had their origin in no less august a source than the very being of the Godhead Himself. Generally I am disposed, on Trinity Sunday, to try to defend the ancient belief of Christendom against the very easy and superficial criticism which would throw it into the discard.

But to-day I want instead to deal with the vision one man had of God, and what it did for his life. I shall be at pains to show you that it makes a difference whether a man believes in God, and what it will do to transform the whole course of his subsequent existence if he catches a genuine vision of the reality of God in this universe. Here, let me say, I am not using " vision " in the technical sense of spiritual appearance to the eye of the inward soul: I mean rather some experience, of hearing, seeing, feeling or discovering which causes a man to acquire an absolute faith " that God is, and that he is the rewarder of them that seek him."

The vision of Isaiah took place " in the year that King Uzziah died." This is not historical detail: it is spiritual setting. Made king at sixteen, reigning for fifty-two years, Uzziah had taken land from the Philistines, and been a patron of agriculture, and been rich in flocks and herds. He was a great king. But he began to feel his own powers. He grew proud and haughty, and one day he went into the temple and with his own hands offered incense which only the priests could offer; and for his proud impiety leprosy broke out upon his forehead at once —and, chased by the priests, he ran out of the temple, and was a leper till he died. The palace changed to the lazar-house. And in the year when this wretched man died, Isaiah saw God.

I expect that Isaiah saw in the sacrilege of the king the representative desecration of the people, and even his own sin. A man given the liberty of a great opportunity, stretching himself to the fulness of his possibility, and then destroying himself by the very freedom which made him great—here was technical dramatic tragedy—here was Adam, and Israel, and all humanity pictured to the life: and because even prophecy itself may be heavily compounded of pride, Isaiah knew by a fearful insight that perhaps he was found in the picture, too. And above the strutting of ostentatious and ephemeral man, above the long panorama of human egotism and impudence, the everlasting Onlooker kept His watch. In the year that leprosy dug a grave for the king's glory, and the greatest human achievement was proved with terrible proof to be temporal, Isaiah the prophet caught a vision of the Eternal.

"I saw the Lord sitting upon a throne, high and lifted up; and his train filled the temple." It does not mean " temple " literally, but " palace." Isaiah may have been standing in the temple, perhaps on the spot where Uzziah sinned; but the vision is of the throne of heaven, and the robes of God fill the spacious courts about Him. The foreground is the Jerusalem temple, fading and shading off into the eternal dwelling of God Himself. In the temple the king had sinned. In the temple Isaiah's conscience had been roused and stirred. Naturally in the temple, with his feet standing upon its rock while his mind scaled the heights of heaven, came the vision of God.

And there is a choir of heavenly beings round about Him, crying: "Holy, holy, holy is the Lord of hosts: the whole earth is full of his glory." We think of the meaning of holiness to-day, and we intend by it great purity or goodness or active loving-kindness. And that is because the Holy Spirit has been working these two thousand years, changing not only our lives but our language. Holiness originally was not positive but negative: it means only separateness, distinctness and difference from man. It was the function of Israel to clean the idea of God: to purge it of heathen attritions; to lift it above moral imperfections. Just where representative man had sinned, Isaiah beheld Him who is of purer eyes than to behold iniquity. Do not suppose that there is any suggestion of a Trinity in the Trisagion, " Holy, Holy, Holy." The repetition is not theological differentiation, it is religious intensification by emphasis. " The whole earth is full of his glory." Glory is the outwardness of holiness, as Jesus' face shone at the transfiguration.

And at this vision of unseen things, this sight behind the veil, what wonder the rocks beneath his feet seemed to shake at the voices of those heavenly beings, and the house filled with smoke? Let no one think that this is the smoke of the incense of worship—it is the smoke which means the meeting of incompatibles, like fire and water, like sin and holiness. It was smoke which hid sinful man from the sin-scorching presence of the All-holy. He stood embarrassed, abashed, at the personal encounter of God.

And from this holiness he recoiled, saying: " Woe is me! for I am undone: because I am a man of unclean lips, and I dwell in the midst of a people of unclean lips: for mine eyes have seen the king, Jehovah of hosts." Sin always focusses for each of us in the place where we sin characteristically: and as for a prophet speech is the purest of all occupations, so uncleanness of lips, dishonesty or vileness, is the focus of all sin. And then he thought of all the blasphemy and low talking and profaneness of speech the whole length and breadth of the land— and then of all the other sin that held the people— and he confessed for himself and for them, saying that his confession was pressed from him because he had looked into the face of God.

Then comes a picture of the profoundest spiritual significance. One of the seraphim flew towards him with a " live coal " in his hand, which he had taken with tongs from off the altar: the meaning is a " glowing stone," such as was the ordinary means for carrying fire in common homes, the fire that warmed the water or cooked the meal or heated the house. Notice this: there is no temple paraphernalia here, no mediatorial apparatus nor ritual. It is as simple a form of sacrament as when our Lord took bread and wine: Isaiah saw the angel take common fire from off an altar of coals before the Lord. And, as in all true sacraments, there accompanied the outward gesture and act a rational and intelligible word: " Lo, this hath touched thy lips; and thine iniquity is taken away, and thy sin forgiven."

Isaiah belonged to a people who believed passionately in physical sacrifice, he stood on a temple-floor where every suggestion of it was made to him: but the only sacrifice he offered was the sacrifice of a broken spirit, a broken and a contrite heart, and the expression of it in confession. Seven hundred years later another Member of his inspired race by one great act of atonement did away with all physical sacrifice forever, One " who needeth not daily, like those high priests, to offer up sacrifices, first for his own sins, and then for the sins of the people: for this he did once for all, when he offered up himself." But the genius of the spiritual insight of Isaiah foresaw in his vision a day of free and unbought grace, which he had for standing abashed in confession, and waiting upon God.

Now, there are some of you here who by now are saying to yourselves, This man is talking unadulterated mysticism: he is dwelling upon the pious imagination of a man long dead, concerning a fancy which came into his head one day as he stood in the court of the temple after the king had died. Let us come into close grips with something modern and near and pertinent!

And to you I should like to say that the things we have been dealing with thus far are neither ancient nor modern, but eternal. For we have seen a man lift up his head to behold the chaos called life. The human reformer was dead in shameful disease. The people were disorganized and rebellious. A catastrophe lay on Isaiah's hands. He could find no solution upon the face of the earth, and he turned up to God. And looking into the face of God he saw against God's holiness his own sin, against God's perfection his own shame. And he felt abysmally unfit to do anything to retrieve the failure men had made of life. And here are the materials for a single human tragedy upon the profoundest scale. Here is where faith is born, or scepticism. This is where a man turns back to life with the power of the everlasting in his bosom, or the desolation of hell in his heart. The bitter satirists of modern life have gone wrong here where they were baffled in the problem of human reconstruction. Some of our most thorny literary critics were really meant for Isaiahs and Ezekiels and St. Pauls. They are ill-content with life as they find it. They crawl away into their libraries to snarl and carp and bite, because they did not, at some crucial moment in their careers, learn to worship and confess and transform the life about them with spiritual forces. You want something modern, do you? The problem of what to do with a chaotic world ought to be modern enough for you!

And the first thing to do for a chaotic modern world is to get some order in your own chaotic souls. Isaiah stood there in the presence of God long enough to let God sink in. He confessed his own utter need, his desperate guilt and shame. And to such honesty God can respond with the gift of grace, with the helping hand of His extended power. You may think it is mystical moonshine we have been engaged with this last fifteen minutes: but it has been an attempt to traverse with a human soul its turmoil of concern about itself and about mankind, and to show that what a man shall do and be forever is dependent upon how he meets that concern, and whether God, the All-holy, the Eternal, is admitted into the innermost recesses of his life. Nothing can happen through you, modern seeker after human betterment, until something has happened to you and in you. The anarchy of your own spirit must give place to a divine obedience. The first problem in all Israel for Isaiah was Isaiah. And the first problem in all modern America for you is you.

Now, when Isaiah's sin is forgiven, he can discern the deep concerns of God Himself. " And I heard the voice of the Lord, saying, Whom shall I send, and who will go for us? " A man has always a false experience of God who has a solitary experience of Him. Come close enough to God to know the sureness of His touch upon your life, and you will feel, with Isaiah, the throb of infinite and indiscriminate outgoing anxiety for all the whole family of earth. " Whom shall I send? " There is a message for the comfortless and hopeless in the

earth, a message for the proud and the self-sufficient
—who will carry it?   For God has chosen to speak
His greatest messages through others, not through
the thunders out of the blue of heaven, but through
the voices of rational and intelligible men.

" Then said I, Here am I."   A man who has just
looked Almighty God in the face is not in a presumptuous mood.   This is not spoken from self-
assurance, it is spoken from desire to co-operate
with God and fulfil His will.   It is an awesome
thing to be volunteer messenger for God.   But
Isaiah will dare to try it, in the power of the grace
that has come to him.   It was not the mood of a
moment, it was the hue and resolution of a lifetime.
Whether he deals politically with Egyptian and
Assyrian intrigue: or morally with the king or the
unsettled people, there is written forever across his
life: " Here am I."   It is the offer of a self.

And having offered himself, seen himself in relation to God's plan, he definitely asks God for a
commission.   " Send me."   Dare you look into
God's heart, and discern all His infinite compassion
towards the children of men, and then think of the
rebellion of men's hearts, their stony indifference,
their calculating and devilish sin, and offering your
life for a bridge say with him: " Send me "?

And swiftly comes the commission: " Go and tell
this people, Listen and listen—but never understand!   Look and look—but never see!   Make
their mind dull, make their ears heavy and close up
their eyes, lest their eyes see, and their ears hear,
lest their minds understand, and their health be
restored."   How shall we interpret this hard say-

ing? Plainly this is not a picture of God's will, but it is a picture of how men act. A genuine message from God does one of two things: it captures and subdues, or it hardens and enrages. If I stand here in Christ's pulpit and say smooth things to you, nobody will be any the worse or any the better: but if God gives me an authentic message from Himself, and I say the truth to you in all its naked power, it will help some people immensely, and it will anger some people furiously. We are not plastic to anybody's hand, nor was Israel: we come into God's house full of predispositions and already twisted in one direction or the other. Real preaching is not presentation, it is strife: it is warfare with sin and the devil for the lives of men. Isaiah knew what the people would do: he was warned of God, that he might not be surprised when it came to pass.

And for the sin of the people, the sin of disobedience, Isaiah promises judgment. God will make a clean sweep. The land will be desolate and forsaken: it will be repeatedly withered for its sin. But hope lay in a minority: there was a remnant— a few true and faithful and inspired souls who would keep the torch burning, and transmit God's light unimpaired to fresh generations. These are two cornerstones of Isaiah's teaching: destruction of the mass, preservation of what was worth preserving. And it all means one thing: God's own self-vindication through human history. He is not mocked. The nation that tries to do without Him shall surely fall. Prosperity may be but the cloak for rottenness. Let us beware, we who are at ease in Zion, lest such a fate come upon us here in our own beloved and foolish land, so rich, so heedless, so restless for God.

So far as Isaiah was concerned, there was one possible prevention of that judgment having full course: and that was that he could get Israel to listen to him when he told them what God wanted. Isaiah stood between Israel and destruction, if they only knew it. He had the solution in his hands. He was the key to the situation, but whether he could unlock doors with it was dependent upon his own powers of persuasion backed by the grace which found him. It was a situation to make a man quail and run with craven fear. But he did not run. He stood in the breach. He tried to make Israel listen to God. Israel was destroyed, as he said they would be when they did not obey: but the remnant was saved according to his prophecy—and the true remnant of Israel was Christ.

That man was in the thick of the politics of his day. He knew them better than king or people. He saw through events to principles, through practical exigencies to eternal falsehoods and truths. Isaiah's vision of God did not send him into an eremite's cell, it sent him into the market-place and the temple and the gatherings of the people. He was one of the great forces of his time. But it came, not from the pleasure of playing politics, not from the love of harangue or being talked about: it came from catching from God, in his vision, the concern of God for mankind. And that is what a genuine vision of God always does for any man: it sends him into the world to remake life to the best

of his ability in accordance with what he has
learned of God.

Now what about ourselves? We come into God's
house this Trinity Sunday, and sing hymns of
praise and say prayers of petition and thanksgiv-
ing. If we are simple enough, real enough, we may
with the insight of the prophet see the Lord high
and lifted up here in His own house. It will comfort us. It will inspire us. What else will it do?
O my friends, let it stir us and awaken us and dis-
turb us with anxiety for His other children! We
say we are only one. So we are. But one may be
enough, where we are, to save the day.

The other afternoon I was walking through the
Metropolitan Arcade, and a man had in his hand a
great bunch of daisies: and he was giving one to the
elevator man, and one to the watchman, and one to
the policeman. It seemed a very little gift. But I
remembered a field of daisies, standing thick with
flowers somewhere in the country: and this nosegay
for a buttonhole in the city came from the country,
it was a real daisy; and they eagerly seized them,
because they wanted that touch of the country in
the town! So is a genuine Christian wherever you
put him—just one, just a unit, just one man to
stand in the gap. But back of him lie the armies of
the Christians: he stands not alone but backed by
all Christ's fields of Christians.

And the heart of the meaning of Isaiah's vision
is perhaps the heart of the meaning of the Christian
Gospel: that God needs men and cannot do without
them. And that when a man dares to put aside, not
the pride of presumption so much as the pride of

false humility, and say to God, " Here am I: send me," God says: " Go! "

Let us pray:

O God, whom in all ages men have sought and found, and who hast made Thyself known to us through Thy Son and Thy Holy Spirit: Grant us this day a genuine vision of Thee, that beholding Thee we may understand Thee, and understanding may obey Thee, and being obedient unto Thee may fulfil Thy will and have some share in Thy redemptive purpose towards all men. Through Jesus Christ our Lord, whom with the Father and the Holy Spirit we worship as one God, world without end. Amen.

IX

WHAT SHALL WE DO WITH TROUBLE?

" Blessed is the man whose strength is in thee: in whose heart are thy ways. Who going through the vale of misery use it for a well: and the pools are filled with water."—Psalm 84:5, 6 (Prayer Book).

BESIDES what religion has to give to human beings of intellectual and philosophical interpretations of life, it has two plain and practical problems which are always facing it. It has got to give men some power by which to get the mastery over sin, and it has got to help them when they are in trouble to find peace and comfort. Religion is both a strenuous and a soothing thing: and much of our difficulty has arisen from our being strenuous when we should have been comforting, and—perhaps more often—from our being soothing when we should have been drastic instead. We are to think this morning of religion in its power to tide us over the places of sorrow in our life.

I suppose that no man or woman gets past thirty years of age, who lives and thinks at all, who does not have to reckon with sorrow and trouble. We all have our early years of easy optimism, when things are going well with us, and the sky is full of sunlight. We ought to be glad for those years, for sometimes they are the years in which we form our great resolves and set out, with magnificent hope,

9036

toward great goals. But the time will come when something flings itself across our path which seems to chill our hope and put out the fires of our hearts.

We set out upon a plan of work, with that mixture of motives, selfish and altruistic, which is so nearly universal. And we put our heart into it, and work for all we are worth, but, do what we will, the thing begins to drag. It does not seem to be altogether our fault, but a combination of forces some of which we cannot control. And one day we must face it bravely but honestly—*we have failed*.

Or a young man undertakes a large piece of work, which is going to demand of him the maximum of intellectual and physical energy. And one day he begins to feel bad, and a doctor tells him that he must pull out of it all, and go into a high atmosphere, for he finds a spot in his lung: and that man turns from all that he hoped to do, and packs himself off to the country to try to regain his health: and the things he dreams there are full of fear and sadness. Or a family watches two beautiful children grow up, amid every opportunity they can provide, and gives them all the world's best: and finds that they only expect more. One makes a good marriage which does not last very long, because it has got no foundations of religion. The other turns hard as flint, and has no human concern for anything but pleasure. And these two children, who began with so much promise, and still in the eyes of the world appear so well, are disappointments to their parents, who carry in their hearts heavy misgivings whether it would not have been better if the kindness had been tempered with less of the selfish joy of giving to one's own, and more of the iron that makes for character. What sadder thing is there in this world than to be disappointed in those God has given us to be our very own?

Or we see a family, happy in its full circle, each contributing something to the whole life—and then, one by one, they fall sick and wither and drop away like the leaves off a tree, until one alone is left, to try to go on and make the best of it when the world no longer holds much of interest.

It is of no good to keep on with the list. We could picture a thousand such instances, and every one of them would evoke the response of someone in this congregation who had " been there." We live in a lonely and terrifying world. Men seem sometimes to be the playthings of a fortune which has in it neither reason to explain it, nor rhyme to soften it. You have not lived at all if you have come to the conclusion that all is well with the world. You have been sitting back in pudgy comfort where you do not see life as it is, if you do not know what tragedies fasten upon human beings. I wish that you could all see what a minister sees in the course of a week, if he is on his job. The reason we have got such shallow views of what Christ did for the world, and the reason we make Him to be such a smiling cheer-monger is that we do not reckon with the exceeding sinfulness of sin, and the exceeding sorrowfulness of sorrow.

I am not given much to sentimentalizing about trouble, and you will generally hear me say things in this pulpit which imply that most of man's difficulty is of his own making and can be of his own unmaking. I say those things because they are the zone of hope in human life, and because I believe infinitely in man, in his freedom to choose and to carve out a wide destiny for himself if he seek the will of God. But I have seen too much of life not to know that sadness and sorrow are not to be dismissed by any facile gesture of hard-hearted optimism, such as parades all round us these days in a hundred self-deceived cults. Evil is serious business in all its aspects: and sorrow is one of them. You will not glorify God, nor better understand the Christian religion, by minimizing the reality of trouble in this world, for the New Testament nowhere does any such thing. " In the world ye shall have tribulation "—that is the verdict. Now what are we going to do about it?

Everything depends upon how you take it and what you make of it. I am not attempting now any guesses at the question of why sorrow is here, but only into the practical question of what to do with it now we've got it. The whole solution is not a theoretical one, but a practical one. Trouble crushes one life, and softens another: embitters one, and makes another sympathetic, because of the different ways in which it is regarded and handled. I will make a few suggestions which have helped me when trouble was present.

In the first place, see your own trouble in its setting as part of the long tragedy which has everywhere accompanied human life. You are not alone in it. Your age is not alone in its sorrows. I remember going up on a hill beside the Bosphorus one afternoon in considerable distress of mind. And I began to think of the infinite pain which had been suffered in that region where I stood. I thought of Roman legions giving themselves that Constantine might build his capital; I thought of the workmen who toiled to build St. Sophia, and of Justinian's vain cry when the church was completed, " I have conquered thee, O Solomon;" of the splendid folly of the Crusaders, crossing this strait into Asia Minor, never to return again to Europe. Gallipoli was a few hundred miles down the narrows, and the bones of English lads filled a gigantic graveyard, not far from the sea. Across the water lay Asia Minor, where Paul had laboured and preached and worn himself out, more Mohammedan than Christian to-day. Possibly there were more Christians in Asia Minor at the end of his life than there are now. And I began to realize that my own trouble was very small, and must be looked at in the light of all this pageant of pain down the ages, which must have some meaning for human life. Sorrow, like sin, isolates its victims, and makes them believe they are alone in their suffering. I think it is a considerable help to make ourselves conscious of the conspicuous place which trouble and sorrow have been given in human experience. If you believe life is explainable at all, you must dignify the experience of trouble by granting that it has its place and carries meaning.

Second, set your trouble in the light of the Cross of Christ. The best the world ever saw came to this. He did not move serenely and indifferently across the stage of human affairs, scattering roses and smiling His way into men's protecting affec-

tions. The closer He got to meeting the world's
need by showing the world where it stood in its relation to God, the closer did He come to treading
upon the toes of men who would not stand for it,
and who finally brought Him to a criminal death.
It would have been a mockery and a joke on us if
He had come into the world in luxury, when men
are in want; slipped through the world in success,
when men fail; and lived to enjoy the full fruit of
His labours, when men are cut off in the bitterness
of disappointment. If He be God, this had to happen. I should have no use for a God who would
not share this colossal tragedy by coming into it
and bearing it. I should deny Him a fraction of
homage. But He *did* share it, shared the extreme
of it, in ignominy and disappointment and physical
pain. The simplest meaning of the Cross is that
God suffered, and in the end that may be for us,
while here below, the profoundest meaning. When
you suffer, remember that God suffered, and suf-
fers still.

Third, share your trouble. I do not mean share
it for the relief it brings to you to talk about it, for
that may be, after a time, a very selfish thing to do.
I mean, share it where it will create an atmosphere
in which someone else in trouble can share that
trouble with you, so that *they* may find relief.
There are gushing people, moist with piety and
dripping with sentimentality, who find dissipation
in unburdening their troubles on others—plainly
they must learn how to be unselfish with sorrow, so
that they do not force it on all, but also do not with-
hold it from those whom it will help. The sun alone

can set free a ship caught in frozen ice-fields; and
you may keep a heart from breaking if you can
start an ice-floe. The sharing of trouble which is
for our own relief is selfish and sentimental, the
sharing which builds a bridge across into the heart
of another is one of God's benedictions let into
the world.

And, fourth, try to find the meaning in your trouble. Perhaps at the very beginning of trouble, you
may be expected only to hold on tenaciously to old
moorings—to stand it. But as the time runs on,
and pain gives place to peace, you will find that God
has not left you at any time, but has been leading
you through the darkness as well as through the
day. You may find a harshness has been melted
out of you forever because of the sorrow you have
suffered. You may find that your absurd trust in
yourself, and your pride in prosperity or pleasure in
success, has given way to dependence upon God,
and reliance upon Him for all your needs. You
may find that when someone you loved was with-
drawn from you, for the first time you learned to
love humanity: and now you see *your* child in every
child, *your* brother in every man, *your* sister in
every woman. I have seen women left alone in the
world who became mothers and sisters to the world;
and men who became its fathers and its brothers.
There is always a hopeful way of taking trouble: a
dear old saint of God, not far from this church, said
to me, in her illness and weakness a little time ago:
" Now I have time to pray as long as I want for
everybody I want to pray for." You may discover
that, since you have been in trouble, for the first

time in your life you can exercise genuine sympathy: it is easy to coin smooth words to say to people when they suffer, but no word at all is better if they know that you have been through what they are going through, and this alone is to " suffer with " anyone.

I do not believe, my friends, that God sends trouble, or deliberately wills the trouble which comes upon the children of men. Much of it is of our own making, some is due to natural forces in the physical universe to which we belong, some of it I give up trying to understand. But I believe that God *uses* that trouble, turns it to good account, works it into the whole fabric of our lives, and gives meaning to it. When I find a person, as occasionally one does, who still is rebellious after years have passed, still grudges the loss of her child or her husband, still reproaches God for a sorrow He did not will, but is anxious to guide and use, I believe that this person is nursing a sorrow for a kind of morbid joy which comes from the clinging to it. You cannot seek the meaning of a sorrow while you hug it to yourself, and will not give it to God to shed His light upon. You must let Him make something of it, or you have yourself been guilty of causing yourself injury, and cannot blame Him if you turn sour and grow hard. You have done it because you refused to find the meaning for yourself. You remember in *Pilgrim's Progress,* where Christian goes through the Valley of Humiliation: and the story says: " This Valley of Humiliation is of itself as fruitful a place as any the crow flies over: and I am persuaded, if we could hit upon it, we might find somewhere hereabouts something that might give us an account why Christian was so hardly beset in this place."

Thus to read sorrow in the light of the sorrows of others, and of our Lord Himself—to allow sorrow to make us more sympathetic than we could have been without it—to see what may " give us an account why we were so beset in this place "—is to go through the vale of misery and use it for a well. The kind of faith which interprets experience in this fashion finds that the " pools *are* filled with water," water enough for us to bear out and give to a thirsty world full of men who are like as in a desert. It looks back upon all the events of life and says that God has wondrously led, and that all things do work together for good to them that love Him. It is no Christianity which tries to make good out of evil, and says that sorrow does not exist: neither is it Christianity which is overwhelmed and crushed by sorrow. It *is* Christianity which finds the hand of God in all experience. It was Jesus who said: " In the world ye shall have tribulation." But He also said: " Be of good cheer; I have overcome the world."

Let us pray:

Father, who dealest gently with Thy children, even when we know it not; teach us to know that nothing but our own disobedience can take us out of Thy hand, and help us to trust ourselves and those we love to Thy loving care at all times. Be thou for us a light in the darkness and joy in all our grief. Through Him who giveth us the victory, our Lord Jesus Christ.

X

UNDISTRACTED LOYALTY TO CHRIST

" If I will that he tarry till I come, what is that to thee?
Follow thou me."—John 21:22.

NO character more steadily maintains throughout the gospels his clear-cut, dominant traits
than Simon Peter. From the beginning to the end
he is the same impulsive, generous, independent,
strong-headed, meddlesome nature. And in the last
chapter of St. John all those characteristics are
recapitulated.

You are all familiar with the story. Simon, con-
sulting no one, announces that he is going fishing—
and the rest follow. In the morning, after a night
without success, Jesus standing on the shore calls to
them to cast their nets on the right side of the ship.
This they do, and they take in a large catch—they
counted them, and there were a hundred and fifty-
three. Simon plunges into the water, unable to get
to the Master quickly enough, and to show Him
their success.

Possibly there was something a little breathless
and unsubstantial about all this protestation of loyalty and attention. After breakfast, He took Simon
alone, and pressed three times upon him that earnest question, whether he really loved Him—and
three times told him what he did would speak
louder than what he said.

Then, turning quickly to the future which they should soon face without His visible presence, He warned Simon what should come: " When thou wast young, thou girdest thyself, and walkedst whither thou wouldest: but when thou shalt be old, thou shalt stretch forth thy hands, and another shall gird thee, and carry thee whither thou wouldest not."

There is hardly any young man who has had any slight experience of religion at all, and who considers the future calmly, who does not realize that matters may look differently when health begins to wane, when obligations begin to tie him hand and foot, when the undeveloped sides of his nature will stick out like a clay-pit in a meadow, and circumstances envelop him in an unbreakable clutch. Perhaps there is no more sobering thought in the world than to wonder whether the religion of our youth is dependent upon happy activity, upon favouring circumstance, upon the buoyancy of first enthusiasm,—whether in the grey days of decline our soul will still travel lightly when our limbs grow stiff.

Yet it is in the midst of this solemn conversation, directed at him alone, a man whose imagination must have seen in a quick flash what Jesus warned him of—it is here that Simon Peter, with consummate spiritual impropriety, looks round and catches sight of the Beloved Disciple, and says to Jesus: " What about him, Lord? " And Jesus comes back with a swift reply to that inquisitive and impertinent question: " If I will that he tarry till I come, what is that to thee? Follow thou me."

There lies profound meaning in Jesus' ready rebuke to the spiritual wool-gathering and preoccupation involved in Simon's question. (The meaning is that there is no more insidious enemy to Christian discipleship than idle curiosity and inquisitiveness into questions which are suggested by discipleship but have no direct relation to it.) There is a place in the Christian religion for thought, for the intellectual faculties to play across the whole complex experience of life, to recognize fact as fact, to cut away superstition which always lies near to the truest religion, and to prevent us from accepting with the intuitive part of us something which the reasonable part of us must reject. But there is no place in the Christian religion for perpetual quibbling about questions which do not bear upon the major and immediate issues of life.

Jesus sends down His command, through the centuries, to go into the ends of the earth and preach His Gospel to every creature. In our souls we know that there is no other religion so good as His, because there is no other life so good as His. But we begin wondering about all the Mohammedans and Hindus and Confucianists and Buddhists that ever lived in ages gone, and our response to His practical command is an abstract question: " Lord, what is going to happen to the souls of all these people in kingdom come? There are good people amongst them. Surely you will not consign the whole lot of them to brimstone and perdition. What will you do with them? " And Jesus says: " All souls are mine. I know where men have been true to the flicker of light that was given them. You stand in the blaze of the Light of the World,

wondering whether their light is as great as Mine.
What is that to thee?   Follow thou Me."

Jesus calls to men to group themselves together
in His fellowship, the Church.   It is the body of
Christ.   It is the brotherhood of believers, and
ideally the only genuine brotherhood in the world.
And we say: " But, Lord, the Church is full of
hypocrites.   I know a man who made a great pro-
fession of Christ, and then took what didn't belong
to him, and then lied to get out of it.   Is that religion?   I know people that go to church, and come
out no better than they went in: is that religion? "
And Jesus says: " What is that to thee?   Follow
thou Me."

Someone sets out to live a Christian life.   And,
for all the joy and adventure of it, there is a good
deal that is hard about it, too.   And the long process of sanctification, the toning-up of the whole of
life in accord with the Spirit of Christ, begins to
wear on us and tire us out.   And then looking
round, like Simon, we see another disciple who just
takes to religion like a duck to water: things seem
to go well, his life looks like a steady crescendo and
progress, he is not devilled as we are by inner misgivings and haunting fears, and we begin to say:
" Lord, why does this person get along so much
more easily than I?   Why do others have a fortu-
nate temperament, while I worry?   Why am I tried
by sorrow and suffering, while they go free? "   And
Jesus says: " What do you know of all the inward
struggles of another life?   What business is it of
yours to complain against God, about the fortune of
another?   What is that to thee?   Follow thou Me."

Or we grow worried about someone we love. Let us say that a younger member of our family gets tremendously interested in Christ and His work. We pine and sigh about the youth of to-day being irreligious—and then in the next breath we lament that our youth has gotten *too* religious. And we wonder what will happen to them if they keep on with this thing. They may give their lives to it, and have very little to live on. They may give up the advantageous marriage we had hoped for, and go and be single, or marry some consecrated soul we never heard of. A number of parents that I know are in a stew over what vital religion may do to their children. And to them Jesus is saying: " The tenderest human ties are yet tenderer to Me. I know every need of your child. Your very worry may break the stream of power by which I can reach that child through every hour of need. What is all that to thee?   Follow thou Me."

Now and then I come across someone who is terribly concerned at what is happening to Christianity in our day. They do not lay the emphasis where it ought to be laid—on the undistracted loyalty of every man and woman to Christ—and work towards that—but they go trotting about spreading a miasma of fear and distrust and prejudice against some section of Christians, or some development with which they are not in sympathy. How often does one hear from some distressed soul about the harm the Roman Catholics are doing, their political activities, and their unbreakable system. Or some very clever intellectual spends any amount of powder blowing up the position of the Fundamentalists.

Or some conservative soul ties up the atheists and the communists and the Bolshevists and the liberal Christians in one big bundle, and wants both Church and state to cart them out into the harbour and throw them overboard.

Jesus did not attack the dangers of His day in that fashion. He sought the undivided loyalty of converted hearts to Himself. He never worried where He could not help. And He says to you: " Do not deal with symptoms, but with causes. Get to men's hearts, and change them, and your society will clear up. Give over your atheistic fears and anxieties about other people's errors. What is that to thee? Follow thou Me."

How many people, as they contemplate the possibility of starting to live the Christian life, want to see the end from the beginning, want to know at the outset just what will be the cost and the outcome. Will this inevitably bring me happiness? May I have to cut my connections with my friends? Would I have to pull out of the business, if I found something shady in its operations? May I hold on to the minor self-indulgence which I love?

Or again, how often they ward off the fundamental issue of deciding for Christ by running up numberless bypaths which lead nowhere. Many a man sits opposite to me in conversation, asking vague questions about Christianity which if they were answered would not alter by a fraction the smallest detail of his life, trifling over irrelevant abstractions while Christ stands in the midst waiting for his choice. And I believe Jesus says to men like that: " I chose a path which began on the bright slopes of Galilee, and closed on a dark hill outside Jerusalem. Shall not the servant tread it still? Leave off your fears for your own future, and your footless questions about interesting spiritual abstractions. What are they to thee? Follow thou Me."

One of the commonest questionings which arise in connection with religion is the question of why some good life is plagued with sorrow. A saint lies stricken on a bed of pain. An upright man and woman lose their child, and life goes out with the loss. A fine young spirit, with infinite possibilities, is snuffed out in a motor accident. The mother of young children goes out of her mind, and leaves a home behind her withdrawal more desolate than if she were dead. I do not believe Jesus could wish us never to ask, " Why? " He asked His own Father, " Why? " from the Cross. But He did not spend His life in futile quibbling and questioning about evil: He did His best to do away with evil and supplant it by good. I think it is true that we do not know the *whole* story of anybody's life but our own: they may need chastening, reminding, softening, testing in ways we know nothing of. We generally can account for the events in our own life, if we wait long enough for God to work through His whole plan. But it is idle to speculate and wonder, where we cannot know all the facts. We may destroy the very faith which would help another to interpret his sorrow helpfully, if we ourselves are unbelieving about it. And Jesus says to us: " What is that to thee? Follow thou Me."

One could go on with instances like these for half

a day. I know many a half-convinced life that will never get any further conviction while these purely external matters of curiosity hold sway over their minds. No sooner does a green blade of faith spring up in their souls, than one of these extraneous questions stands ready with the shears to cut it down. Even when a believing human soul can give good reason in reply to the question, that kind of a mind retreats to take up another question, forever asking and never deciding.

I want to say to you again, I am not pleading for irrational faith. A faith without intellectual foundation is not going to stand for long: and a faith you can't look at honestly is superstition. But I am saying that there are moods of distracting inquisitiveness and curiosity in which, if they are persisted in, it is easy to pull up the roots of the firmest faith. There are many questions of interest, questions which whet our wits and feed our imaginations, questions the philosophers have left unanswered, and which yet have nothing to do with the immediate business of living well.

The Christian solution to these questions, or to the deeper problem of existence out of which they all arise, is a unique one. Jesus says that all knowledge of this interior, spiritual world is best had through first forming a loyalty to Himself which is undistracted by any prior considerations whatever: and that in the attachment with Him there comes a kind of understanding in which the questions which really matter in life are made clear. " I am the light of the world," is His claim, " he that followeth me shall not walk in the dark-

ness, but shall have the light of life." There is a
loyalty, there is a holy preoccupation with Jesus
Himself, which becomes a climate in which irrelev-
vant questions no longer clamour for solution, and
in which the questions which concern the practical
prosecution of life find answer. That is one of the
deepest and one of the most blessed of the experiences of religion.

Jesus asks from us an attachment unlike anything else on this earth. There is no human being
to whom we can give ourselves with the utter cer-
tainty that in the very giving there is sure illumination and blessing. He says to all the ages,
" Follow Me," with the imperiousness of certain
authority. He will not brook any turning aside to
consider any lesser issues: that attachment is primary, and all else must find its place in subserv-
ience to it. Jesus asks you to " go it blind " with
Him. He asks it because He knows that only so
will you ever gain your sight.

There lie a thousand questions in the minds of
people in this church this morning, questions bearing upon religion if not arising out of it. Many of
you wonder what God can do with your own futile
past, and others look into the future with fear.
Another is bothered with the wages of sin, or the
dread of age, or the approach of sickness, or the
possibility of enormous disappointment, or the obligation to a distasteful duty—or just the age-old
everlasting and ever-present problem of the evil in
the world, which no religious man can blink without
nursing a lie in his soul. It is a temptation for us
all to muse and fret about these things, all the while

that Jesus is laying upon us the command to follow. Like Simon, we are ever looking over our shoulder at these things, and so drawing away our attention from Him to them.

But it has been the cumulative experience of the finest spirits who have ever crossed this earth that when they turn back to Christ from these distracting and upsetting and irrelevant questions, and concentrate their attention upon the one gigantic attachment to Christ, living all their lives upon this straight-line loyalty to Him, there is guidance and grace for each separate problem which arises, the tangled skeins of life come straight, and there hovers about that one tremendous loyalty itself such radiance of illumination as can never be found elsewhere on this planet.

Give over, then, I ask you, your secondary questionings and your irrelevant inquisitiveness into matters which are not pertinent to what you ought to do next. Foster and encourage the spirit to follow Christ, at all costs, whithersoever He leads. And you will find, what many more of us have found, that " in his light we shall see light," and in His straight path we shall not stumble.

Let us pray:

O Master of the world: who art still lovingly and imperiously calling us away from all the distractions of sin and curiosity which divide our loyalty to Thee: Keep us from the sin of idle questioning and help us so to put our trust in Thee that we may learn by following, and see, by utter surrender, all of the truth which we need. We ask it in Thy Name. Amen.

XI

THE HIGHER REACHES OF CHRISTIAN EXPERIENCE

" I will lift up mine eyes unto the hills."—Psalm 121:1.

PROBABLY the most difficult problem which any idealistic way of taking life must encounter is the problem of where to adapt, and where to refuse to adapt, to that mixture of sordidness and possibility which we call human nature. Religion is dedicated to the proposition that there is a spirit in man: and that however strong or evil his instincts may be, they can be brought into line with the high desires of the spirit.

Christianity passionately believes that. And yet again and again our religion has suffered the same decline to which all our human affairs are subject. We let it slip down into comfortable counterfeits. We tend—the best of us—to compromise with human nature. We say, with our lives if not with our mouths, that human nature is too weak a thing to expect that it can be lifted up to the level of New Testament Christianity: so we had better adapt Christianity till it better fits human nature. We conform to our surroundings, we compare our religion with the rest of the congregation, we take colour from our companions who belong to the world, we keep up with the neighbours in clothes and houses. In the very solitude of our own hearts, we admit to ourselves that we " cannot always live on the heights." How many times have you heard people say that?

Yes, we succumb to our own human nature. David Harum says some folks have more human nature than others—and we belong to the some that are afflicted with lots of it.

To-day, as we look into the archways of a fresh year of life, perhaps it will help us to get above the common levels of Christianity as we know and live it, and to think about the high places where we may still climb in the year that opens before us and the time that is left to us. Few of us would venture to say that the past year did not contain great spiritual neglects and even great spiritual failures. One feels something close to fear as he considers the cycle of the years, running swiftly on, and sees what a short distance he has moved since he passed the last milestone.

I know that for myself I feel there are whole great areas where my own Christianity is weak, and where I want to lift and deepen my own experience. I always try to preach to myself when I am speaking aloud to you, but especially to-day I shall be talking of levels of spiritual living far above those to which I have grown accustomed in the touch-and-go of ordinary living. I shall speak, not so much of places where I have been, as of places where I should like to be, and where I should like to go in your company through this next year of spiritual pilgrimage. Let us this morning " lift up our eyes unto the hills," and consider several of the high places of the spirit.

I should like to live always in the high place of *faith*. I do not mean the low hills of assent to inherited theological propositions, but the high hill of such trust in God as literally transfigures the earth. I mean the faith which refuses ever to consider any situation a trap, but views each one as a crucible in which some creative event may take place—the kind of faith which set St. Paul to work in prison as gaily as in the market-place, which sees advantages wrapped in limitations, and man's extremity as God's opportunity which He will not fail to improve.

I mean the faith which sees through the outwardness of sorrow to its inwardness, and finds a meaning for the deepest loss: as a friend wrote to me but this week of the death of her husband, " I think I have got to the point of realizing *why* the person I loved most in the world had to go. With him alive I was too happy and too contented. I'm afraid I should never have made any *real* effort after truth. It was one of those instances where the ' good ' (and oh, how good it was!) was the enemy of the best." I mean the faith that cannot be shaken out of its inward harmony and tranquility by any outward misfortune or neglect or hostility: but that has a foundation in another world, utterly independent of what man can do unto it.

I mean the faith which is sure of the final conquest of good over evil—sure of it because the quantity of evil is outweighed by the quality of good, and because God is God. And the faith which sees in immortality the inevitable outgrowth of the kind of life which Jesus Christ makes possible in this world.

I should like always to live in the high places of *love*. Love that allows nobody to stand outside its view, builds no artificial fences between people, sees men's hearts and not their clothes or their colour, and looks on them somewhat as God looks on them. Love that is never uncomfortable in the presence of incompatibles, but with ingenuity brings together into fellowship divers kinds of people who would usually not understand each other, love which is a great reconciler of those whom the crusty custom of the world has divided. Love that rejoices in the success of those who are our rivals, is fair to the truth of those who are our critics, is patient of those who wilfully misunderstand us.

Love that is brave enough to call sin sin, and to conclude all men under sin: and then to refuse to believe that there is a soul anywhere that cannot be saved. Love for those that irritate us, foolishly take our time, needlessly harry us about trifles, are stupid about taking a hint. Love that always sees people and situations as they lie in the mind of God, big with potentiality, no matter what the situation be. I am convinced that love like that will wear some of us out, and tax us beyond human power: it crucified Christ, but it set going a new force in human life.

And humility—the high place of *humility*. Someone will say it ought to be a low place for humility: but I think not. Genuine humility cannot be attained by avoiding pride: it can only be attained by discovering gratitude. The truest humility in the world is that of the man who has been lifted up by God, carried above his sins, given peace for his pain

and joy for his crying; and who, standing on the
strong rock, thinks not of the security of his own
position but of the mercy of God for putting him
there. Yes, humility is a high place—a very high
place indeed. There are human door-mats who
feign humility but do not have it. They are culti-
vating it as a virtue: and the cultivation of humility
as a virtue is almost a vice. Let them experience a
great deliverance, or really know the salvation of
God in their souls, and their humility will grow out
of their sense of obligation and gratitude.

Let us all try this coming year to dwell so much
upon what God has done for us that we may develop an ever-present thankfulness to Him. And
then we shall refer all the joy and success of our
life to Him and not to ourselves. And that is hum-
bleness. I do not want mock-humbleness, the obse-
quious and snivelling kind: but the humility which
is born of meditating upon that great thought,
" What hast thou that thou didst not receive? "

Another high place where I would like to live
always. I should like always to make an *impression for Christ,* and not for myself, upon every life
I meet. There are lives in the world obviously possessed. One feels in them both the constraint and
the liberty of a great Other, with them at all times.
That impression would be made often by words, for
what a man loves most, that he talks about. But it
will be made, too, by the subtlest attitudes, by the
things he reads and doesn't read in the newspapers,
by the books on his table, by the recreation he
chooses, by the way he talks to the telephone oper-
ator, and says good-morning to the elevator man in

his office. You know as well as I do that there are
people who live that way twenty-four hours in the
day, and they are not saccharine and effusive people, they are as often quiet and restrained people.

Christ works through us according to the nature
He has given to us. One of us will touch people by
buoyancy and enthusiasm: another will touch them
by the possession of evident inward peace. One
will witness for Christ by radiant health and happiness: and another will show Him forth by patience
in illness. It is possible, when we meet people, to
be relaxed, sensitive, generous of time, responsive,
ready to change our plans to meet their needs: and
through a life thus ready and at liberty from itself
Christ can and does shine. Surely it would be to
live on the heights if we could succeed in never giving a misimpression for Him: if we could literally
reflect Him in every word and act and thought.

And then there is another high place of Christian
experience. ˙ It is the height a man reaches when
prayer becomes the climate of his life. Not a ritual,
not a habit, not a last resort, but a climate wherein
a man's soul draws breath. One comes increasingly
to believe in the reality of a spiritual kingdom, as
high above the animal kingdom as the animal is
above the inanimate—a kingdom with its own laws
which supersede the laws that science understands
in the two lower kingdoms. When a human soul
lives continually in that kingdom, the common
events of life are seen in a glow of significance,
coincidences turn into Providences, frustrations
into opportunity, and miracle becomes the order of
the day. There is a higher ether which if a man

breathe, all his normal gifts are lifted into super-human power, as unlettered men were empowered to write the most immortal books in the world.

There is nothing to be wondered at if some who make this kingdom their home, see beyond into the World of Reality at times through the eyes of their souls, and come back to say that they have seen a vision of Christ and eternity. From the height of that mountain, many things are visible beyond which are hidden from our eyes as we walk below in the valley. And in that kingdom, the communication of the will of God to our finite minds becomes, in the truest sense, natural: it is expected, we are quiet enough to hear, and obedient enough to understand; our wills slip over into God's will and become one with it. This is not an unscalable height: I know lives that live there, and would God we might all join them and dwell with them " in heavenly places by Christ Jesus."

Now, it will do us only harm if we are content to look up to these high places from a distance, and then stay where we are. I think that it was Chesterton who once described the mood of most of us with comic accuracy: " I will lift up mine eyes unto the hills, but I will not drag my carcase thither." We need to stake fresh claims for ourselves on those high places during this new year, and to take new ground. And we had better begin to make the ascent by roads which are accessible to us.

Let us determine at all costs that we shall master our besetting sin this year, and put its domination behind us. What holds us back from faith and love and living for Christ and communion with God?

Generally the thought of our utter unworthiness, which is another way of saying our sin. To each of us there is a familiar form of it, that besets and tortures and bedevils us: and which is the gateway to a train of discouragement and loneliness and more sin. And the reason we fail with the mastery of it is usually that we do not definitely give it up, or believe that we can give it up: but when we break it, keep the memory of its possibility in one corner of our minds, remembering that we can always go back to it. Let us claim for ourselves that great promise, in the fourteenth of Romans, " Sin shall have no more dominion over you."

Let us anew turn over to God all our possessions for His use. The only possible excuse for our being well cared for is that what we have we really share with those in need. It is easy to have a comfortable house which we meant to use that way, and then to draw into its quietness and enjoy its peace for ourselves. The last thing most Christian people ever surrender to God's immediate guidance is their bank-account: they will not dare to let the Holy Spirit preside while they are writing checks. They will even be humanly generous, but to allow God complete control in what they do with what they possess requires an absoluteness of dedication which they will not make. Let us at least be tithers, but let us not be content until God has it all. For Jesus knew the opportunity of possessions, but He knew their danger, too, to wall the life away from the very need it ought to satisfy. We cannot live on the high places without committing all our possessions to God.

Let us stake a claim in Bible study this year. Let us resolve that next New Year's will find us thoroughly familiar with one great book—say Isaiah, or St. John's Gospel, or Romans. The depth of spiritual life is partly measured by our understanding of the Word of God. Modern Christianity is full of good works, but we are weak on scholarship and on deep Bible study.

Also, let us do some real spiritual reading this year. Get hold of Dick Sheppard's *Impatience of a Parson,* and you will find, not I think an adequate solution but a very acute diagnosis of the present state of religion. Bishop Temple's *Christ the Truth* is solid reading but illuminating: so is Hocking's *Human Nature and Its Remaking*. One of the profoundest books that has appeared in recent years is Rudolph Otto's *Idea of the Holy*—not light reading, but a deep shaft sunk into spiritual truth. Our Christianity is shallow for the most part. Let us deepen it with knowledge.

And then let us take another road—a hard road for many. Let us promise God that we shall choose a group of people, and do our best, by prayer, by the gifts of books, by influence, to reach them decisively for Christ this next year. I mean that for every one of you, no matter what predilections or prejudice you may have about " personal work." Do it as you choose, so you do it with the help of God. But do not do it slip-shod. Do not leave it till next December. Do not complain about your shyness: forget it in the urgency of the love of God. Get them on your hearts and in your prayers. Pray for God's solution to all their problems, for

God to open the door to you. It is wonderful how prayer changes the face of a relationship.

I am convinced that many a Christian will never walk on the high places of his faith just because he will not learn how to share his faith with others. I know you weren't brought up that way, some of you: neither was I. I had to learn it. But I would not go back to that old buttoned-up religion, when I was afraid to say a word for Christ, not for anything! This city is ripe for a great awakening. Your friends, who say little, think much. Get busy. Determine that you will be of some use to God through this coming year, or find out what is the matter.

Yes, the hills are high, but they are nearer than we thought, because there are roadways that lead up to the top. Some of you have never seriously thought of changing your comfortable religion, and going up higher. God give us all this New Year's Day the mind to forsake the compromises of the years that are flown, and to seek the heights with Christ.

Let us pray:

Father, forgive the cold love of the years. Our souls have always looked up to the high places, and known that they were our rightful home. But we have been tied and bound by fear to change our ways. Lift us up by the glory of Christ's hope for us, and help us to make the ascent to the life Thou wouldest have us to live. Through Jesus Christ our Lord.

Printed in the United States of America